LIGURIA

PAUL BLANCHARD

LIGURIA
Updated chapter from *Blue Guide Northern Italy*

Published by Blue Guides Limited, a Somerset Books Company
Winchester House, Deane Gate Avenue, Taunton, Somerset TA1 2UH
www.blueguides.com
'Blue Guide' is a registered trademark.

ISBN 978-1905131-77-8

The first ever Blue Guide, *London and its Environs*, was published in 1918 by two
Scottish brothers, James and Findlay Muirhead. The first edition of *Blue Guide
Northern Italy* was compiled by them and L.V. Bertarelli in 1924. Subsequent
editions were revised, compiled or written by the Muirhead brothers (1927, 1937);
Stuart Rossiter (1971); Alta Macadam (1978, 1984, 1991, 1998) and Paul Blanchard
(2001, 2005). This chapter was updated by Paul Blanchard.

The author and publisher have made reasonable efforts to ensure the accuracy of
all the information in this book; however, they can accept no responsibility for any
loss, injury or inconvenience sustained by any traveller as a result of information
or advice contained in the guide.

Every effort has been made to trace the copyright owners of material reproduced
in this guide. We would be pleased to hear from any copyright owners we have been
unable to reach.

Statement of editorial independence: Blue Guides, their authors and editors, are
prohibited from accepting payment from any restaurant, hotel, gallery or other
establishment for its inclusion in this guide or on www.blueguides.com, or for a
more favourable mention than would otherwise have been made.

Town plans © Blue Guides
Maps: Dimap Bt © Blue Guides
Prepared for press by Anikó Kuzmich.

Cover image: Camogli © Annabel Barber/Blue Guides

www.blueguides.com
'Blue Guide' is a registered trademark.
We welcome reader comments, questions and feedback:
editorial@blueguides.com

About the author

Paul Blanchard is a Florence-based writer, visual artist, art historian, speaker and landscape theorist. Two editions of *Blue Guide Northern Italy* have been published under his curatorship. He is also the author of *Blue Guide Southern Italy*, *Blue Guide Concise Italy* (the latter also available in digital format) and the Blue Guide chapter *Trentino & The South Tyrol*, available digitally and in print-on-demand form.

CONTENTS

Introduction

Stretching between the French frontier and the borders of Tuscany, Liguria comprises the narrow strip of land lying between the Mediterranean and the Maritime Alps and the Apennines, and a small part of the Po River basin beyond the watershed. Because the mountains shelter it from winter winds, the region enjoys an exceptionally mild climate. Delicate plants from the Mediterranean basin, California, Chile, South Africa and Australia thrive along city streets, in the countryside, and in formal gardens. In the western section of the region vegetables and flowers are grown out of season for export to northern markets, and everywhere olives and grapes flourish on the steep hillsides. The gentle climate, combined with the grandeur of Liguria's rugged coastal scenery and the attractions of the sea, have for over a century drawn visitors from less fortunate places, especially during winter. This tradition gives Liguria's many coastal resorts a timeless quality that is difficult to find elsewhere in Italy, and is perhaps the region's most attractive feature.

HISTORY OF LIGURIA

It is hard to say when the first humans came to Liguria. At the Caverna delle Arene Candide near Finale Ligure, archaeologists have found stone implements dating back at least 25,000 years, as well as several graves. The oldest is that of a fifteen-year-old boy who died more than 20,000 years ago. Ten thousand years later the cave became the burial site of 23 individuals, whose tombs make up the world's earliest known necropolis. The cave cannot be visited today, but the finds can be seen in the superb archaeological museum in Pegli, Genoa's elegant western suburb.

Liguria receives its name from the *Ligures*, a loose grouping of Neolithic peoples who lived in village settlements on the Mediterranean coast from Spain to Tuscany in the 1st millennium BC. They established early contact with the first known navigators of the Mediterranean, the Phoenicians and Greeks, and in the 3rd century BC they allied with Rome against Carthage. In the 2nd century BC the region came under the dominance of Rome, whose fortunes it followed until the fall of the Empire. After brief Lombard and Frankish rule, the city of Genoa emerged as a leading power in the 11th century. Its sailors liberated the coast from the attacks of Saracen pirates and captured their strongholds of Corsica and Sardinia. After loosening their ties with the Holy Roman Empire and establishing a self-governing republic, its citizens went on to build one of the principal maritime and commercial powers of Europe, establishing a great colonial empire that extended as far as the Crimea, Syria, and North Africa.

Despite numerous conflicts with competitors, notably Pisa and Venice, the Republic of Genoa remained free and independent until the 17th century, when the growing might of the Ottoman Empire, the transfer of trade with America to Atlantic ports, and the maritime hegemony of Spain brought its rapid decline. In 1684 the capital surrendered to the French king Louis XIV, after heavy bombardment, and in 1768 the Genoese sold their rights to their last remaining colony, Corsica, to France. Napoleon seized Genoa in 1796, and formed the Ligurian Republic in 1802. This soon became a French province, but in 1815, after Napoleon's fall, Genoa was joined to Piedmont by the Treaty of Vienna. It went on to become a stronghold of the Risorgimento, under the leadership of Giuseppe Mazzini, a native. Garibaldi led his expedition against Sicily from here in 1860. In the new unified Italy, Genoa became a major port, rivalling Marseilles in France.

CULTURE AND LANDSCAPE

The Italian Riviera, Liguria's rough, picturesque coast to the west and east of Genoa, is known as the Riviera di Ponente and the Riviera di Levante, respectively. Today, both areas display evident signs of wealth: clean, orderly towns with well-tended public spaces, yacht harbours bristling with the masts of expensive sailboats, and stately villas built at a time when it was not important to fill a lot corner to corner. It may seem surprising, at first, that the modern richness of this once poor, harsh land is linked as much to the fertility of the soil and the clemency of the climate as to the productivity of industry. This is not to say that industry is lacking: Genoa and La Spezia host Italy's leading shipyards, La Spezia is Italy's largest naval base, and Savona is a major centre of the Italian iron industry. Not so long ago, chemicals and textiles were important, too: Genoese sailors of the 17th century were the first to wear robust cotton trousers dyed with indigo—in French *bleus de Genes*. Two centuries later the combination was chosen by San Francisco merchant Levi Strauss to clothe American gold miners. In recent years, however, reconversion from heavy industry to high technology and business services, and a steady increase in tourism, have made the environment the region's most valuable asset. Ecosystem management has become the key to future economic growth, as sun-seekers and new businesses alike are drawn to the region by its fine climate and ample recreational opportunities.

And, of course, by its rich and pervasive cultural heritage. That Ligurian culture is distinctive, is everywhere evident: buildings are painted in rich, creamy colours, ranging from deep sky blues to russet reds and dark ochres, posing a chromatic contrast to the surrounding land- and seascape that has long fascinated painters and photographers. For those unimpressed by colour, there is form: nowhere is *trompe-l'oeil* decoration used so effectively on building exteriors as in Liguria. The endless, ingenious variations on faux rustication, faux sculptural decoration, faux windows and doors exceeds imagination and gives charm to even the simplest of villages. Add to Liguria's architectural attractions the almost sinful luxuriance of its gardens, and you begin to understand why so many 19th- and 20th-century artists and writers chose to live here: the sophistication lent to this land by centuries of interaction between humans and their natural environment is simply unmatched elsewhere.

ART AND ARCHITECTURE

Liguria does not have a memorable school of visual art, as Tuscany or Umbria, Venice or Naples have. Genoa has always been receptive to foreign ideas, and interestingly it was influence from outside Italy that inspired the art of its most fruitful time, the 17th century. Through its close commercial links with the Netherlands, the city acquired many Dutch and Flemish paintings. Rubens and Van Dyck were in Genoa in the early part of the century; other influence came from Umbria and Lombardy (especially Caravaggio). The best sculpture in Liguria also comes from outside the region—from the workshops of the Pisano family of Tuscany and the Maestri Comacini, stonecutters from Lombardy whose work adorns many churches. The most distinctive feature of Ligurian religious architecture, the black-and-white striped façades of its churches, is believed to have been brought from the Holy Land by the Crusaders.

Despite the lack of a strong historic tradition (or perhaps because of it), modern Liguria is extremely important on the art scene—thanks to the presence in the region of major personalities such as painter/sculptor Lucio Fontana (arguably the most important Italian artist of the mid-20th century), writer Eugenio Montale (Nobel Prize for Literature, 1975) and architect Renzo Piano (Royal Institute of British Architects Gold Medal 1989, Pritzker Prize for Architecture 1998, American Institute of Architects Gold Medal 2008).

The Argentine-born Fontana produced the first of his ground-breaking ceramic sculptures in the seaside resort of Albissola, wedding his Modernist avant-garde vision with a tradition of craftsmanship that has flourished in this area for centuries. (Coincidentally, Fontana was busy in Albissola at roughly the same time Picasso was working in Antibes and Vallauris, Léger in Biot and Yves Klein in Nice—all just across the French frontier, on the Côte d'Azur.) Fontana died in 1968, but the production of original, distinctive ceramics continues along the coast between Albisola and Savona. Today, if you want to take home something distinctively Ligurian, the brightly coloured freehand designs broadly known as Savona faience are the things to buy—though they don't come cheap.

Eugenio Montale, journalist, music critic, novelist and, above all, poet, used natural images of the Ligurian coast to express his feelings: in one interview he claimed his poems were as 'rough and dry' as the rocky headlands of the Cinque Terre, where he spent his summers. His first volume of poetry, *Cuttlefish Bones*, published when he was just 29, and the *Collected Poems* are available in English and are essential reading for anyone seeking to grasp the essence of Liguria.

Until recently, Renzo Piano was best known as co-designer (with Richard Rogers) of the Centre Georges Pompidou in Paris (1971–7). Now he is likely to achieve even greater fame for the California Academy of Sciences in San Francisco or the New York Times Building in New York, two revolutionary designs that maximise energy conservation. His architectural practice, Renzo Piano Building Workshop, has its headquarters in Genoa and is responsible for the brilliant redevelopment of two waterfront neighbourhoods: the Old Harbour and Punta Nave.

Last but not least, a word must be said for Ligurian *patrons* of the arts, for it is they who commissioned the lovely villas and gardens of the 19th and early 20th centuries, and who continue to make Liguria a place where new ideas in architecture, urban and territorial planning, and visual and performing arts flourish

Genoa

Genoa is built on an unlikely site: the irregular seaward slopes of an amphitheatre of hills. Today it is an important container port, but at the height of its powers it ruled the destinies of the entire seaboard, of Corsica and Sardinia, and of much of the eastern Mediterranean. It preserves many relics of an ancient, honourable history, including the numerous palaces and magnificent art collections of its great maritime families (many still in private hands). Today town planners and private individuals have adopted a bold stance, preferring to take risks in order to assure that the tradition of fine building that characterises the historic city centre (declared a UNESCO Heritage of Humanity site in 2006), should continue. Renzo Piano (a native *genovese*) and other internationally known Italian architects (Carlo Scarpa, Aldo Rossi and Ignazio Gardella, to name a few) have been invited to build here. Admittedly, the tangled assortment of buildings tumbling down the mountain to the Ligurian Sea is not the city by the Arno: it is far less pretty. It is also plagued by mistakes from the past: the city expanded rapidly after the Second World War and town planning was chaotic—for example, the city is cut off from its waterfront by an elevated expressway, like Seattle, or San Francisco before the 1989 earthquake. For precisely these reasons, Genoa poses a greater challenge to architects and planners than more harmonious cities do; in the near future, as its urban renaissance nears completion, it may also offer greater rewards to visitors.

The old city, clustered round its harbour, is still a most interesting district, with its tall houses in steep, narrow alleys or *caruggi*, some less than 3m wide. Work is proceeding slowly, if not steadily, to restore these dark streets, with their quaint old-fashioned shops. Some important restorations and new buildings were completed for the celebrations in 1992, which marked the 500th anniversary of the American expedition of Genoa's most famous native, Christopher Columbus. A project to revitalise the area of the old harbour—entrusted to Renzo Piano—is still underway.

The position of Genoa, at the northernmost point of the Tyrrhenian Sea and protected by mountains, has given it a lasting maritime importance. The original Ligurian inhabitants of the site established early contact with the first known navigators of the Mediterranean, the Phoenicians and Greeks, and there was a trading-post here in the 6th century BC. In the 3rd century BC Genoa allied itself with Rome against the Carthaginians, and when the town was destroyed by the Carthaginians in 205 BC, it was rebuilt under the Roman praetor Cassius.

Roman connections were not entirely severed until the arrival of the Lombards in 641. In the succeeding centuries the fleet of Genoa drove back the attacks of Saracen pirates and expelled the seafaring Arabs from Corsica and Sardinia. Sardinia was taken with the help of Pisa, and its occupation led to two centuries of war, which ended in the final defeat of the Pisans at Meloria (1284). With this success began the acquisition of Genoa's great colonial empire.

Power in the Genoese Republic was in the hands of the *podestà* and the *capitani del popolo*, with intervals of submission to Emperor Henry VII (1311–13) and to Robert of Anjou, King of Naples (1318–35). In 1340 came the election of the first doge, Simone Boccanegra, whose story is told in one of Giuseppe Verdi's most famous operas. Petrarch, on a visit in 1358, described the city as *la superba* (the proud), a name used by numerous subsequent travellers to Genoa. Chaucer was sent to Genoa in 1372–3 by Edward II, to arrange a commercial treaty with the maritime republic. Continual strife between the Genoese patrician families made the city an easy victim to the rising military powers, and it had a succession of foreign rulers in the 15th century. In 1528 Andrea Doria (1466–1560), the greatest of the Genoese naval leaders, formulated a constitution for Genoa that freed the city from foreign rule, though it established an oligarchy at home. Changes in the balance of power in the Mediterranean in the 17th century brought the decline of Genoa (and of all Liguria), as outlined in the Introduction.

GENOA TRIVIA

• Population of 1.5 million in the metropolitan area.
• A vertex of the Milan-Turin-Genoa industrial triangle.
• Important university town and high-tech research hub.
• 42km long (from Vessina to Nervi).
• 1km high (city limits range from sea level to 1183m, at Monte Reixa). There are funicular railways linking the top and bottom of the town.
• Traditionally Europe's most vertical city (the highest point of the republican wall circuit was Forte Sperone, on the summit of Mount Peralto, 489m).
• Subtropical (Köppen Cfa) or Mediterranean (Köppen Csa) climate, depending on location. The temperature range in town is just 6/7°C daily (in all seasons), and 16° annually (hottest month/coldest month).

IMPRESSIONS OF GENOA

The Genoese manner...is exceedingly animated and pantomimic; so that two friends of the lower class conversing pleasantly in the street, always seem on the eve of stabbing each other forthwith. And a stranger is immensely astonished at their not doing it.

Charles Dickens, letter to John Forster, 20 July 1844

The people here live in the heaviest, highest, broadest, darkest, solidest houses one can imagine. Each one might 'laugh a siege to scorn'. A hundred feet front and a hundred high is about the style, and you go up three flights of stairs before you begin to come upon signs of occupancy. Everything is stone, and stone of the heaviest—floors, stairways, mantels, benches, everything. The walls are four to five feet thick. The streets generally are four to five to eight feet wide, and as crooked as a corkscrew. You go along one of these gloomy cracks and look up and behold the sky like a mere ribbon of light, far above your head, where the tops of the tall houses on either side of the street bend almost together. You feel as if you were at the bottom of some tremendous abyss, with all the world far above you. You wind in and out, and here and there, in the most mysterious way, and have no more idea of the points of the compass than if you were a blind man. You can never persuade yourself that these are actually streets, and the frowning, dingy, monstrous houses dwellings, till you see one of these beautiful, prettily dressed women emerge from them—see her emerge from a dark, dreary looking den that looks dungeon all over, from the ground away halfway up to heaven. And then you wonder that such a charming moth could come from such a forbidding shell as that.... There may be prettier women in Europe, but I doubt it.

Mark Twain, The Innocents Abroad, 1869

Genoa is the crookedest and most incoherent of cities; tossed about on the sides and crests of a dozen hills, it is seamed with gullies and ravines that bristle with those innumerable palaces for which we have heard from our earliest years that the place is celebrated. These great edifices, with their mottled and faded complexions, lift their big ornamental cornices to a tremendous height in the air, where, in a certain indescribably forlorn and desolate fashion, overtopping each other, they seem to reflect the twinkle and glitter of the warm Mediterranean. Down about the basements, in the little, dim, close alleys, the people are for ever moving to and fro, or standing in their cavernous doorways or their dusky, crowded shops, calling, chattering, laughing, scrambling, living their lives in the conversational Italian fashion. For a long time I had not received such an impression of human agglomeration. I had not for a long time seen people elbowing each other so closely, or swarming so thickly out of populous hives.

Henry James, 'Italy Revisited', 1877, in Portraits of Places, 1883

The dock-front of Genoa is marvellous. Such heat and colours and dirt & noise and loud wicked alleys with all the washing of the world hanging from the high windows.

Dylan Thomas, letter to his parents, 5th May 1947

THE CITY CENTRE

From the 10th to the 13th century, Genoa was built as a dense mass of extremely narrow streets and tall buildings, and it is the urban development of these centuries that gives the innermost core of the city's historic centre its distinctive atmosphere.

In the Middle Ages property values were understandably high in any walled city—where the walls provided the only guarantee of physical security—but here topography had a role, too, the steep slope of the terrain driving land values even higher and making construction arduous and costly. Tall elevations, therefore, became a necessity. Later, in Genoa as in other European cities, architecture and urban planning came to focus on more spacious buildings, streets and squares, reaching proportions considered appropriate to mass society in the 20th century. What is unique about Genoa is the degree of contrast between the city's ancient core and the modern (17th-century and later) neighbourhoods around it

PIAZZA DE FERRARI AND THE PALAZZO DUCALE

For the Genoese, both the physical and spiritual centre of the city is Piazza De Ferrari (*map Genoa East, 11; Metro De Ferrari*). Here numerous main roads converge on a beautiful large fountain whose recently restored jets form a surging white cupola surrounded by alternating rings of light and dark stone, in their turn surrounded on three sides by only slightly less spectacular ancillary fountains. Behind Augusto Rivalta's Garibaldi monument (1893) rises the city's opera house, the **Teatro Carlo Felice**, rebuilt on a huge scale by Aldo Rossi in 1987–91. The first theatre, designed by Carlo Barabino in 1828, was destroyed by fire in 1944, although its Neoclassical porch survived. The new building includes a massive rectangular tower for the complicated stage machinery. The interior is just barely this side of kitsch: rather than boxes, the stone-faced houses of a *borgo marinaro* flank the parterre, and the vaulted ceiling is sprinkled with lights in a way that evokes a starry night sky. In defence of this Postmodern figurative extravagance one should say that the stone is Bardiglio blue marble, which ensures exceptionally good acoustics. The theatre was inaugurated in 1828 in the presence of Carlo Felice and Maria Cristina of Savoy, with a performance of Bellini's *Bianca e Ferdinando*, the story of an usurped throne regained; bearing in mind that Genoa had lately been assigned to the realm of Savoy (by the Congress of Vienna, 1815) after centuries of fierce independence, the choice may have a significance all its own. Certainly the theatre is rumoured to be filled with the restless spirits of the Dominican friars whose monastery was razed to build it—or, according to another story, of the ghost of the young Leila Carbone, condemned for witchcraft and burned on this spot in 1580.

In front of the theatre is the Neoclassical **Accademia Ligustica di Belle Arti** (1827–31), designed by the same architect as the theatre, Carlo Barabino. A gallery on the first floor of this famous art school (*open Tues–Sat 2.30–6.30, www. accademialigustica.it*) contains paintings, sculptures, prints and drawings by Ligurian artists of the 13th–19th centuries as well as a small but beautiful collection of ceramics. The highlight is Luca Cambiaso's intense, contrasty *Christ before Caiaphas*, considered the most dramatic night scene painted in Italy in the 16th century.

Opposite are the flank of Palazzo Ducale, seat of the Doges of Genoa, and a palace built as offices in 1923 by Cesare Gamba. Behind this, in Piazza Matteotti, the Baroque church of **Gesù e Santi Ambrogio e Andrea**, built 1589–1606 by Giuseppe

Valeriani, has a sumptuous, colourful interior with frescoes by Giovanni Battista Carlone and altarpieces by Guido Reni (*Assumption*, south aisle) and Peter Paul Rubens (*Circumcision*, over the high altar and *St Ignatius Healing*, north aisle)

Palazzo Ducale, a magnificent large building of various periods, surrounds Piazza Matteotti. The left wing, originally the palace of the Fieschi (the noble family that produced Pope Innocent IV), was the seat of the *capitano del popolo* after 1272, and from 1294 the meeting place of the *comune*; it became the residence of the doges from 1340 onwards. Andrea Ceresola ('Il Vannone') made some radical changes c. 1591–1620, adding the spacious vestibule with an airy courtyard at either end, and the palace was almost completely redesigned by Simone Cantoni in 1778–83, when it was given its Neoclassical façade. On the upper floors are the Salone del Maggior Consiglio and the doges' chapel, frescoed by Giovanni Battista Carlone. Exhibitions are held here, and there are rooms dedicated to jazz, cinema, poetry, photography and robotics, each with its own programme of activities. There is also a café/restaurant.

INTO THE *CARUGGI*

Via San Lorenzo leads from the Palazzo Ducale into the labyrinth of steep narrow alleys, or *caruggi*, that is old Genoa.

SAN LORENZO

The Romanesque-Gothic church of San Lorenzo (*map Genoa East, 11*), consecrated unfinished in 1118, modified in the 13th–14th centuries, and altered again during the Renaissance, is Genoa's cathedral. Arriving from Palazzo Ducale you skirt the south flank, walking by some Roman sarcophagi, a 15th-century Grimaldi family tomb, and the Romanesque portal of San Gottardo. The **façade** has doorways in the French Gothic style (thought to be based on the coeval portals of Rouen cathedral and those, slightly earlier, of Chartres) guarded by lions added in a 19th-century Gothic Revival restoration. The **campanile** at the southwest corner was completed in 1522; the one at the opposite corner is unfinished, terminating in a plain loggetta of 1447. On the north flank are the 12th-century **portal of San Giovanni** and quite a few more classical sarcophagi.

Dark Corinthian columns set the tone of the **interior**. The proportions were altered when the nave roof was raised in 1550 and the cupola, designed by the renowned Baroque architect Galeazzo Alessi, was added in 1567. Frescoes of the *Last Judgment* and the *Glorification of the Virgin* by an anonymous early 14th-century artist fill the lunette over the west door of the nave. In the south aisle, beside a British naval artillery shell that damaged the church without exploding in 1941, is a marble relief of the *Crucifixion* of 1443, likewise by an unknown hand. The story of the *Judgement and Martyrdom of St Lawrence* is told in the ceiling frescoes of the presbytery, by Lazzaro Tavarone. The chapel to the right of the high altar holds a *Vision of St Sebastian* by Federico Barocci, and the chapel to the left of the high altar has ceiling and wall paintings by Giambattista Castello ('Il Bergamasco') and Luca Cambiaso, respectively. The carved choir stalls date from 1514–64.

Despite the cathedral's dedication, Genoa's patron saint is not Lawrence (nor George, whose red cross on white field is the emblem of the Republic) but John the Baptist, who is honoured by the **Cappella di San Giovanni Battista**. Designed by Domenico and Elia Gagini (1451–65), this grand chapel harbours statues by Matteo Civitali and Andrea Sansovino (1504), a baldacchino of 1532, and a 13th-century French shrine for the saint's relics, all behind a richly decorated front. The handsome Renaissance tomb of Giorgio Fieschi (d. 1461), by Giovanni Gagini, graces the adjoining chapel. The **treasury** contains ancient glass, copes, the Byzantine *Zaccaria Cross* and precious reliquaries, all displayed in superb stone and concrete vaults designed in 1956 by the Modern architect Franco Albini.

SAN DONATO TO SANTA MARIA DI CASTELLO

From Palazzo Ducale the Salita Pollaiuoli descends southwest into the old town, with its narrow dark *caruggi* and their tall houses. Some charming portals survive in this district, in white marble or black slate with occasional reliefs of St George. There are also numerous Baroque street tabernacles housing sacred images. The little Romanesque church of **San Donato** (*map Genoa East, 11*), probably founded in the early 12th century, has a splendid polygonal campanile and a doorway with Corinthian columns and shallow, striped-stone porch. In the basilican interior are an exquisite late 14th-century *Madonna and Child* by Nicolò da Voltri and a magnificently detailed triptych of the *Adoration of the Magi* by Joos van Cleve.

On Piazza Sarzano rises the pink façade of the **Museo di Architettura e Scultura Ligure di Sant'Agostino** (*map Genoa East, 11–15; Metro Sarzano– Sant'Agostino, open Tues–Fri 9–7; Sat, Sun and holidays 10–7*), housing the city's collection of architectural fragments, sculptures, detached frescoes and ceramics. The museum occupies a 13th-century Augustinian monastery and church, the only one of the great 13th-century Genoese churches to preserve its origin Gothic interior. The exhibition spaces were designed between 1962 and 1992 by Albini Helg Piva and Albini Associati, successors of the architectural firm established in 1930 by Franco Albini; the use of finely-worked glass, steel, wood and stone embodies the firm's approach to architecture as craft 'streamlined' by industry. Highlights of the collection include, on the first floor, fragments of Giovanni Pisano's funerary monument of Margaret of Brabant (wife of the Holy Roman Emperor Henry VII, she died in Genoa in 1311), a painted Crucifix by Barnaba da Modena, and other sculptures in wood and marble; and on the second floor, 15th-century black slate architraves with reliefs of St John the Baptist and St George. There are also carved masks by Taddeo Carlone; detached frescoes by Luca Cambiaso; some fine sculptures by Gian Giacomo Della Porta, Silvio Cosini, Filippo Parodi, Pierre Puget and Antonio Canova, as well as an unusual group of 15th-century English (Nottingham) alabaster carvings (artworks of this kind were salvaged from English churches by Genoese merchants and mariners after the Reformation). The church of Sant'Agostino, with a graceful campanile and spire, is now the museum's auditorium.

Santa Maria di Castello (*map Genoa West, 10*), a Romanesque church with 15th-century Gothic additions, occupies the site of the Roman castrum and preserves some Roman columns. Inside, on the west wall, is a late 15th-century fresco of the

Madonna and Child with Sts Dominic and Peter Martyr, by Lorenzo Fasolo, from the destroyed church of San Domenico; in the south aisle, altarpieces by Aurelio Lomi (*Martyrdom of St Blaise*), Pier Francesco Sacchi (*Madonna Hodegetria*, showing the Christ Child as 'the Way') and Bernardo Castello (*Martyrdom of St Peter of Verona*). Next to the new altar is a wonderfully expressive wooden Crucifix of c. 1100, the *Cristo Moro*, the sanctuary holds a marble group of the *Assumption of the Virgin* by Antonio Domenico Parodi and there is a *St Rosa of Lima* by Domenico Piola in the chapel to the left of the sanctuary. The baptistery contains a 15th-century polyptych, some ruined 15th-century frescoes and a Roman sarcophagus. The sacristy has a beautifully carved portal (inner face) by Giovanni Gagini and Leonardo Riccomanni (1452).

The Dominican **monastery** (1445–1513) has pretty frescoes in the loggia of the second cloister, possibly by 'Justus de Alemania', the German painter who signed and dated (1451) the *Annunciation* on the wall. In the upper loggia (view of the harbour), with Roman and medieval capitals, is a tabernacle of the Trinity by Domenico Gagini and a detached fresco in monochrome of the *Vision of St Dominic*, attributed to Braccesco. The old library has a polyptych of the *Annunciation* by Giovanni Mazone (1470; one of only two works known by this local artist). The museum (*open daily 9.30–12 & 3.30–6.30*) contains liturgical items, sculptures (notably a painted marble *Madonna and Child* by Domenico Gagini), paintings (*Pala Ognissanti*, a painting showing Flemish influence, signed and dated 1513 by Ludovico Brea), miniatures and a reconstructed monastic cell.

SOME REPUBLICAN PATRICIAN HOMES

Piazza San Matteo, a few paces north of the Palazzo Ducale, was created in the 12th century when it was surrounded by the mansions and church of the Doria family, the former bearing the striped stone pattern that only the noblest of families were authorised to use on the façades of their homes. **San Matteo** (*map Genoa East, 11*), founded in 1125 but rebuilt by the Doria in 1278, has a black-and-white Gothic façade with inscriptions recounting the glorious deeds of its patrons. The interior was redesigned in 1543–7 (for Andrea Doria) by Giovanni Angelo Montorsoli. The sanctuary has a splendid array of architectural and figurative sculptures and stuccoes designed by Montorsoli and executed with the help of Silvio Cosini; the pair also produced the high altar, the choir loft and the dual pulpits. Giambattista Castello ('Il Bergamasco') and Luca Cambiaso painted the scenes from the life of St Matthew in the nave, and Anton Maria Maragliano carved the poignant wood group of the *Deposition*. Montorsoli designed the crypt and staircase, with their marbles and stuccoes, for the tomb of Andrea Doria. An archway on the left of the church leads to the cloister (1308–10), by Magister Marcus Venetus.

Opposite the church is the **Casa di Lamba Doria** (no. 15), built in the 13th century, with a portico. The **Casa di Andrea Doria** (no. 17) was built for Lazzaro Doria in 1468 and presented to the famous admiral by his native city in 1528. No. 14 is the **Casa di Branca Doria**, about whom a story is told. According to contemporary chronicles this Doria scion married his daughter Caterina to the son of Michele Zanche, lord of Logudoro in Sardinia, only to murder his father-in-law at a dinner party given in the unfortunate man's honour. The motive of the crime was, most ignobly, money: Zanche was immensely rich and influential, and Branca seems not to have thought twice about usurping his power and taking possession of his property. So foul was his deed that Dante sent him straight to the ninth circle of the Inferno while Doria was still alive. Understandably, Doria was not pleased by the treatment the poet reserved for him and had his thugs beat him up when he next visited Genoa—or so the 16th-century historian Oberto Foglietta reports. In all fairness it must be said that Michele Zanche was hardly a paragon of virtue: Dante placed him in the pit of swindlers, immersed in boiling pitch. The author of the *Divine Comedy* seems not to have held a high opinion of the Genoese in general: in the same canto where he tells the story of Branca (XIII) he writes, *Ahi genovesi, uomini diversi d'ogne costume e pien d'ogne magagna, perché non siete voi del mondo spersi?* (Ah, Genoese, men different in every way and full of every vice, why are you not cast to the far corners the world?). On moonless nights, it is said, you can see Branca's ghost roam the little square: it is he who stains the last north column of the church nave blood-red.

Piazza Banchi (*map Genoa West, 6; Metro San Giorgio*) is where the money-changers had their tables (*banchi*) until the end of the 18th century. The **Loggia dei Mercanti** was designed by Vannone in 1589–95. It was turned into an exchange—the first of its kind in Italy—in the 19th century. The restored, centrally planned church of **San Pietro in Banchi** was designed by Bernardino Cantone and built by Giovanni Ponzello and Vannone (1581).

Via San Luca leads north from the square. This was the main street of the city from the Middle Ages to the 18th century, when it was the principal place of residence of the great Genoese families. It is now full of shops and offices. The little church of **San Luca**, rebuilt in 1626, is a fine example of Genoese Baroque architecture, with an interior frescoed by Domenico Piola. The frescoes show the *Crowning of the Virgin* (in the dome), *Jael, Judith, Job* and the *Prodigal Son* in the corbels, *Stories of St Luke* in the presbytery and the choir and allegorical figures of the *Virtues*, in monochrome, on the west wall and in the transept. On the nave ceiling are *St Luke Baptising the Neophytes* and the *Supper at Emmaus*. There are also some fine sculptures, by Filippo Parodi (marble *Virgin with Angels* over the high altar) and Giovanni Benedetto Castiglione ('Il Grechetto': wooden *Deposition of Christ* and *Nativity*, possibly his finest work).

Beyond, Vico Pellicceria leads right to Piazza Pellicceria, with Spinola family townhouses. No. 1 is now the **Galleria Nazionale di Palazzo Spinola** (*map Genoa West, 6; open Tues–Sat 8.30–7.30, Sun and holidays 1.30–7.30*). This 16th-century mansion became the property of the Spinola family in the early 18th century, when the collection of paintings was formed. It is a particularly interesting example of a patrician Genoese residence that preserves more or less intact its 17th–18th-century decorations, as well as its furniture and paintings. The first-floor Salone has a ceiling frescoed by Lazzaro Tavarone (1615) and bronzes by Ferdinando Tacca. The Primo Salotto contains works by Stefano Magnasco, Giovanni Battista Gaulli (Il Baciccia) and Giovanni Battista Carlone. The Secondo Salotto contains a portrait of Ansaldo Pallavicino by Van Dyck, another of him with his father by Domenico Fiasella (who also painted him as doge; this portrait is in the dining room) and a portrait of a lady by Bernardo Strozzi. The second floor was decorated for Maddalena Doria (wife of Nicolò Spinola) in 1734. The Salone has another ceiling fresco by Tavarone, completed in the 18th century by Giovanni Battista Natali, who also painted the walls as a setting for paintings by Domenico Piola, Gregorio de Ferrari, Luca Giordano and Bernardo Strozzi. The Primo Salotto still has its 18th-century decorations and furniture. The Secondo Salotto displays paintings by Guido Reni, Luca Cambiaso, Valerio Castello and Bernardo Strozzi. The *Four Evangelists* are by Van Dyck. The Terzo Salotto has works by Carlo Maratta, Bernardo Castello, Giulio Cesare Procaccini and Francesco Vanni. The *Virgin in Prayer* is by Joos van Cleve, who stayed in Genoa in 1515–20 and again in 1525–8. The charming Galleria degli Specchi (1736) was probably designed by Lorenzo de Ferrari, who painted the vault fresco. The Quinto Salotto has paintings by Marcantonio Franceschini, a portrait of Paolo Spinola by Angelica Kauffmann, and 18th-century furniture.

The 'authentic palazzo' ends here. The third and fourth floors are occupied by the paintings, sculpture, porcelain and textile collections of the Galleria Nazionale della Liguria. Highlights are an *Ecce Homo* by Antonello da Messina, an equestrian portrait of Gio Carlo Doria by Peter Paul Rubens, a portrait of a lady with a child by Van Dyck, a statue of *Justice*, part of the funerary monument of Margaret of Brabant, by Giovanni Pisano, a portrait of Scipione Clausone by Tintoretto, bronzes by Giambologna, and two small female portraits by Pierre Mignard in exquisite 17th-century frames (one by Filippo Parodi).

THE STRADA NUOVA (VIA GARBALDI)

In the mid-16th century, at the height of their commercial and financial influence, the wealthy aristocratic families that held power in the Genoese Republic decided to construct a new quarter in the upper part of the city that would express their prominence in an unmistakable way. This project materialised as the *Strada Nuova* (today Via Garibaldi; *map Genoa East, 7*), which was built in 1551–83 at the foot of the hills in the northern part of the old town. This 'new street' was 250m long and 7m wide (more than twice the width of medieval streets); it immediately became the city's most exclusive address, the setting for the splendid palaces and the theatre of the lavish entertainments of the leading families of the Republic. In 1601–18 a second *Strada Nuova* was built further west by members of the Balbi family (the present Via Balbi; *map Genoa West, 2*), and in 1778–86, a third new street, the *Strada Nuovissima* (today Via Cairoli; *map Genoa West, 6*), was opened up to link the two earlier neighbourhoods.

Via Garibaldi, which extends between Piazza Fontane Marose and Piazza della Meridiana, just half a kilometre from Genoa's beautiful new waterfront promenade, was added to UNESCO's World Heritage list in 2006. Its design is attributed to the architect Galeazzo Alessi (1512–72), who also designed several of the palaces. The architects of the other palaces were Giambattista Castello ('Il Bergamasco', 1509–69), Bernardino Cantone and the brothers Domenico and Giovanni Ponsello.

Due to the slope of the site, the design of each palace was tailored to fit its particular location. A few characteristics are generally shared, however: most are three or four storeys high and combine an elaborate entrance hall with spectacular courtyards, open staircases and loggias overlooking luxurious gardens arranged on different levels. Nearly all have illusionistic façades with painted and/or stone elements, and interiors adorned with stuccos and frescoes. This same grand style of construction was taken up again in the palaces of the second *Strada Nuova*, built for Giacomo and Pantaleo Balbi (1618–45), Agostino Balbi (1618–70) and Stefano Balbi (1643–55). The Savoy rulers chose Stefano Balbi's mansion as their residence in Genoa, and that palace is now known as Palazzo Reale.

A senate decree of 1576 placed the aristocratic palaces on the three *strade nuove* on an official list—the *Lista dei Rolli*—which obliged owners to give hospitality to distinguished guests of the Republic during state visits. The Rolli list was divided into three categories: the first, which included the most luxurious palaces, was reserved for royalty and high clergy, the second for governors and nobles, and the third for guests of lesser standing. The palaces of the *strade nuove* were invariably listed in the first category.

The model of the Genoese palaces was exported to other states in Italy and the north, thanks to the work of artists such as Rubens (who published drawings of the palaces), Giorgio Vasari, Vincenzo Scamozzi and Joseph Furttenbach. It profoundly influenced Baroque town planning in Germany, Britain and the Netherlands.

Today Via Garibaldi is one of the most handsome streets in Europe. Most of its magnificent palaces have been painstakingly restored, and to stroll from one end of the street to the other is an unforgettable experience. With this in mind, the street has been pedestrianised. Three of the palaces are superb museums.

GENOESE ART AT THE TIME OF THE GREAT PALACES

The greatest name of the 16th century is Luca Cambiaso (1527–85), a precocious talent who frescoed the Palazzo Doria (now the Prefettura) aged only 17. The geometric forms he uses in his drawings almost foreshadow Cubism. Cambiaso's influence carried over into Lazzaro Tavarone and Bernardo Castello, though their derivative Mannerist style lacks true originality. Genoa's most fruitful time was her Seicento. The city has always been receptive to foreign ideas, and interestingly it was the influence from outside Italy that inspired the art of this period. Through its close commercial links with the Netherlands, the city acquired many Dutch and Flemish paintings; Rubens and Van Dyck were in Genoa in the early 1600s; other influence came from the Urbino-born Federico Barocci and from Caravaggio. The greatest native artist of the age is Giovanni Benedetto Castiglione (c. 1610–65, known as Grechetto), who is said to have invented the monotype. He was much influenced by the Netherlandish painters, and was in turn much admired by Tiepolo. Bernardo Strozzi (1581–1644) took monastic vows as a young man, but cast aside his habit and went on to leave his artistic mark on the city. Domenico Piola (1628–1708) was a fresco artist of some genius. Also important is Domenico Fiasella. Though not a notably great artist, he was much sought-after in his day, and extremely prolific. He, like so many of his contemporaries, was a confirmed Caravaggist.

PALAZZO ROSSO

Via Garibaldi 18. Map Genoa East, 7. Open Tues–Fri 9–7, Sat–Sun 10–7. Café/ restaurant and shop.

This magnificent building of 1671–7 was erected for Ridolfo and Gio Francesco Brignole Sale by Pier Antonio Corradi and decorated in 1687–9 by Gregorio de Ferrari, Domenico Piola and others. Like Palazzo Bianco it was bequeathed to the city (in 1874) by Maria Brignole Sale. The collection includes fine portraits of the Brignole family by Van Dyck. There are also works by Dürer, Guercino and Lodovico Carracci. The Genoese School (Bernardo Strozzi, Giovanni Benedetto Castiglione) is well represented.

PALAZZO BIANCO

Via Garibaldi 11. Open as Palazzo Rosso.

Built for the Grimaldi c. 1565 and enlarged after 1711 by Giacomo Viano for Maria Durazzo, widow of Giovanni Francesco Brignole Sale, the palace was presented to the municipality in 1884 by Maria Brignole Sale. It contains part of her collection of paintings, together with later acquisitions, with some particularly beautiful Flemish and Dutch works. The gallery was excellently rearranged and modernised in 1950 by Franco Albini. Only the outstanding pieces are on view. Highlights include a number of works by Luca Cambiaso (*Madonna and Child with St Mary Magdalene, Christ at the Column, St Jerome, Madonna della Candella*). The masterpieces of the collection are Hans Memling's *Christ Blessing*; Jan Provost's *Annunciation*; and Gerard David's *Madonna della Pappa*, c.1510. The greatest highlights are Van Dyck's *Christ and the Coin*, which shows the artist's stylistic debt to Titian; Rubens' celebrated *Venus and Mars*, painted in Antwerp between 1632 and 1635; and Caravaggio's splendid *Ecce Homo*, in which a highly symbolic use of light underscores the purity and meekness of Christ.

PALAZZO TURSI (THE TOWN HALL)

Via Garibaldi 9. Open as Palazzo Rosso.

Flanked by raised gardens, the palace was begun in 1568 for Nicolò Grimaldi by the Ponzello brothers, and the loggias were added in 1597 around the magnificent courtyard. Grimaldi was a multi-titled aristocrat as well as a major private banker, his lead client being Philip II, king of Spain and Portugal. Accordingly, the palace is the most sumptuous on the street. It contains the Guarneri violin (1742), which belonged to Genoa-born Nicolò Paganini (1784–1840), as well as three letters from Columbus.

Most of the other mansions in this street can be admired only from the outside, though the courtyards are usually accessible. **Palazzo Podestà** (no. 7) was begun by Giambattista Castello and Bernardino Cantone in 1563, and has a good stuccoed vestibule and a Rococo grotto and fountain in the courtyard. **Palazzo Spinola** (no. 5) has frescoes in the atrium and vestibule (the fine courtyard has been enclosed for use as a banking hall). **Palazzo Doria** (no. 6), of 1563, was remodelled in 1684, with a charming little courtyard. **Palazzo Carrega Cataldi** (no. 4) is by Giambattista Castello and Bernardino Cantone (1558–60), and has a splendid hall of mirrors (*opened on request*). **Palazzo Lercari Parodi** (no. 3), attributed to Galeazzo Alessi (1571–8), has a portal with two atlantes by Taddeo Carlone (1581). **Palazzo Gambaro** (no. 2) is by Bernardo Spazio (1558–64) and **Palazzo Cambiaso** (no. 1) is by Bernardino Cantone (1558–60).

In the irregular Piazza Fontane Marose (*map Genoa East, 7*) are **Palazzo Pallavicini** (no. 2), begun 1565; **Palazzo Negrone** (no. 4), altered c. 1750; and the 15th-century **Palazzo Spinola dei Marmi** (no. 6), with a coloured marble façade and statues of the Spinola family.

MUSEO DEL RISORGIMENTO, PALAZZO REALE AND VILLA DEL PRINCIPE

Beyond the western end of Via Garibaldi, at Via Cairoli 18 (*map Genoa West, 6*), Palazzo Balbi has an ingenious staircase by Gregorio Petond (1780). Via Lomellini diverges south from Via Bensa to the **Museo del Risorgimento e dell'Istituto Mazziniano** (Casa Mazzini, no. 11; *open Tues, Wed and Fri 9–1, Sat 10–7*). It contains an excellent collection documenting the Risorgimento. The museum is Giuseppe Mazzini's birthplace: he did not live there during his adult life, most of which he spent on the run, so you shouldn't expect to see his study or his writing table. There is the guitar he loved dearly (and played very well, contemporary accounts tell us), as well as documents regarding the Risorgimento (among these, the manuscript of Italy's national anthem, by Goffredo Mameli, another Genoese patriot), the political history of Genoa and the First World War. The museum is an interesting stop for all those who have an interest in early modern European history

GIUSEPPE MAZZINI

'I fought with the greatest of soldiers, Napoleon. I brought to agreement emperors, kings and popes. No one gave me more trouble than an Italian bandit: skinny, pale and ragged, but eloquent as a storm, ardent as an apostle, smart as a thief, casual as an actor, tireless as a lover, whose name is: Giuseppe Mazzini.'
(Klemens von Metternich, *Memoirs*)

'The nation is the home of men, not of slaves.'
(Giuseppe Mazzini, *Ai giovani d'Italia*)

The character that Mazzini (1805–72) stamped upon the struggle against absolutism and foreign domination in Italy is due to his belief in national unity. The country, he believed, could not be reborn except through a profound political, intellectual and moral revolution. The new state thus created would reflect the needs of the entire nation and would be run democratically by all citizens. Any other solution would enable the old evils to survive in new forms, would not be an authentic expression of Italian 'genius', and would not restore to Italy the ability to carry out its mission of civilisation. 'I spoke,' Mazzini wrote in 1861, 'when all were silent. And if the youth of Italy was moved by my words, it is a sign that those words responded to trends that were hidden, but powerful and ingrained.' His thought became the basis of a new political movement in Italy in the second quarter of the 19th century.

Born in Genoa in 1805, Mazzini joined the Carboneria (a secret society opposing absolute monarchy, initially in the Kingdom of Naples and later in northern Italy, France and Spain) in 1827; at the same time he began his career as a journalist and philosopher, producing essays that affirmed the civil function of literature and the social and political commitment of writers. He was arrested in 1830 for his association with the Carboneria and interned in Savona, but in the absence of evidence he was released and forced to choose between exile and confinement to a remote village. He left the country in February 1831 and, after wandering through Switzerland and France, eventually settled in Marseilles. There his contacts with other political activists convinced him that the Carboneria was too limited in vision and too provincial in scope to be a true instrument of revolution. Feeling that the opportunity for change was at hand, he formulated a new political programme and new methods of action, and established a new association, *Giovine Italia* (Young Italy), to carry them out. The key objectives of the new revolutionary organisation were political unity and republican government.

It's hard to grasp the originality of Mazzini's ideas without considering the particular form of religiosity on which he based every real possibility of *revolution*, or human renewal. Only religious thought, he wrote, is able to alter human conduct in a deep and lasting way. What he had in mind was not the thought of institutionalised religion but the moral force, the sense of mission (conceived in earthly terms of human civilisation) that reason cannot arouse without the assistance of faith. This attitude, on which Mazzini also based his critique of the French Revolution and the Enlightenment, drew its general inspiration from Romanticism, and certain specific values (for instance, the notion of a 'brotherhood of man') from the ideas of the French social reformer Henri de Saint-Simon. In Mazzini's view, the mission given by God (or history) to individuals and peoples must be seen in terms of the universal law that drives humankind toward continuous progress. Mazzini considered the Italian Risorgimento as a movement of universal scope. Only the people as a whole can accomplish the mission of freedom and progress because only in the people does God reveal himself and his power. *Dio e popolo* were the foundations of Mazzini's political philosophy; education and insurrection, the basic and inseparable terms on which the struggle was to be conducted.

Mazzini's programme had a force far greater than that of previous secret societies, and Young Italy enjoyed a vast breadth of support, especially amongst intellectuals and the urban middle and working classes. Nevertheless, the failure of the first attempts at insurrection (1833–4) and the harsh repression that followed created serious difficulties. Mazzini fought back by uniting exiles from other parts of the continent, founding Young

Germany, Young Poland and, perhaps most significantly, Young Europe, in Berne in 1834. This did not save him, however, from a profound spiritual, political and moral crisis (the 'storm of doubts'), triggered largely by the blood shed in the name of his ideas. Expelled from Switzerland, he settled in London in 1837, where he reorganised the ranks of Young Italy, sparking a new set of insurrections in 1840. By 1848 these, too, had ended in failure, leading to criticism of Mazzini and doubts about the validity of his claims. In the meantime a new development had come along to pour salt into the wounds of Mazzinian republicans and widen the scope of the struggle against absolutism and foreign domination: a strong moderate liberal movement that set itself the much more modest objective of constitutional monarchy.

Mazzini died in Pisa in 1872, in an Italy unified under the (limited) sovereignty of the House of Savoy. His ideal of a democratic Republic of Italy would be fully achieved only in 1948, in the wake of the Second World War and the disastrous marriage between Vittorio Emanuele III of Savoy and Fascism.

Via Bensa continues from Via Cairoli to **Piazza della Nunziata** (*map Genoa West, 2*), dominated by the 19th-century Neoclassical pronaos of Santissima Annunziata, a church rebuilt 1591–1620. From here the narrow Via Balbi continues uphill towards Principe Station, past many dignified old mansions. On the right is Palazzo Durazzo-Pallavicini (no. 1; now Giustiniani Adorno), by Bartolomeo Bianco, with a later double loggia. Palazzo Balbi-Senarega, opposite (no. 4), is also by Bianco. Since 1803 the University has occupied the palace at no. 5, built in 1634–6 as a Jesuit college by Bartolomeo Bianco.

At no. 10 is the former **Palazzo Reale** (or Palazzo Balbi-Durazzo), designed c. 1650 for Stefano Balbi by Michele Moncino and Pier Francesco Cantone and remodelled in 1705 for the Durazzo family by Carlo Fontana (*map Genoa West, 2; open Thur–Sat 9–7, Sun and holidays 1.30–7, first Sun of the month 9–7*). From 1842 to 1922 it was the royal seat in Genoa and it contains several suites of sumptuously decorated 18th-century rooms in which are a *Crucifixion* by Van Dyck and works by Luca Giordano, Domenico Parodi, Bartolomeo Guidobono and Bernardo Strozzi. The little theatre (Teatro del Falcone), which suffered a direct hit by a Second World War bomb, has been rebuilt and recently reopened as an exhibition space.

VILLA DEL PRINCIPE

Opposite the Stazione Marittima passenger terminal, but with its entrance inland at Piazza Principe 4, the **Villa del Principe** (*map Genoa West, 1; open daily 10–6, www. dopart.it/genova*) is probably the most sumptuous of all Genoa's house museums. The *principe* in question is Andrea Doria (*see below*), who acquired two buildings here in 1521 and had them made into one by Domenico Caranca (1529); Montorsoli may have added the loggia (1543–7) facing the garden. Charles V and Napoleon were entertained here in 1533 and 1805 respectively, and the composer Giuseppe Verdi wintered here from 1877. Still owned by the Doria Pamphilj family, the palace contains frescoes by Perin del Vaga and stuccoes by Luzio Romano and Guglielmo della Porta in the vestibule and on the stairs, as well as portraits of Andrea Doria (by Sebastiano del Piombo) and Giannettino Doria (attributed to Bronzino). Equally remarkable are the tapestries in the Appartamento del Principe, with *Stories of Alexander the Great* (in the Camera di Perseo) and *The Months* (Sala dei Sacrifici), woven in Brussels c. 1525; and those in the Appartamento della Principessa showing the *Battle of Lepanto* (Salone del Nettuno, late 16th century) and *May* and *December* (Sala del Tributo, 18th century).

The spacious High Renaissance garden is a place of unexpected beauty and peace in an otherwise busy and chaotic corner of town; it was restored to its 16th-century form—a joint creation of Giovanni Angelo Montorsoli and Giovanni Ponzello—in 2000.

ANDREA DORIA

Doria (c. 1466–1560) began his career as a mercenary general in the service of Francis I of France. Following a disagreement, he switched allegiances and fought for the Habsburgs instead, reaching an understanding with the Holy Roman Emperor Charles V that however much territory he won for the empire, the independence of Genoa would remain secure. In 1528 he became virtual ruler of Genoa, though he was careful not to dissolve the city state's ancient oligarchical councils and senate. He was also admiral of the Genoa fleet, and went to Spain's aid against the Ottoman Turks. A gifted seaman, Doria has gone down in history as the man who discovered how to sail against the wind. His portrait by Bronzino (Brera, Milan) shows him in the guise of Neptune, self-assured and semi-naked, a sturdy trident standing in for what the drapery barely conceals.

THE OLD HARBOUR

Piazza Caricamento (*map Genoa West, 6*; Metro San Giorgio) faces the Porto Vecchio, Genoa's old harbour. Here is the Gothic **Palazzo di San Giorgio** (restored in 1992), begun c. 1260 and extended towards the sea in 1570. The façade facing the harbour was frescoed by Lazzaro Tavarone in 1606–8. Once the palace of the *capitani del popolo*, it became in 1408 the seat of the famous Banco di San Giorgio, which was largely responsible for the prosperity of the city from the mid-15th century onwards. Here citizens could lend money for compound interest and the idea of cheques was introduced. It is now occupied by the Harbour Board.

Across the road is the **Molo Vecchio**. To get there you have to walk under the intrusive raised highway, the Sopraelevata Aldo Moro, a short-sighted 1960s' solution to the traffic problems created by the city's long, thin crescent shape. The quay was begun in 1257 by the Cistercian friars Oliverio and Filippo; the imposing **Porta Siberia**, designed by Galeazzo Alessi, dates from 1553. The area was redesigned by Renzo Piano in 1992: he converted the old cotton warehouses into a congress centre and created an open-air space on the quay for spectacles and fairs, next to the **Bigo**, an unusual metal structure that serves as a 'crane' for a lift from which there is a panoramic view (*opening hours vary; see www.ticketacquario.it and* *click on 'Bigo'*). In the warehouse area are the **Museo Nazionale dell'Antartide** (*open Tues–Sun 10–6*) documenting Italian scientific expeditions to Antarctica and giving visitors an experience of conditions there; and the **Città dei Bambini** (*open Tues–Sun 10–6*), a hands-on science and technology museum for children aged 2–12.

The **Aquarium** (*open Jan–Feb 9.30–8 or 9–30–9; March–June and Sept–Oct 9–8 or 8.30–9; July–Aug 8.30–10.30, www.acquariodigenova.it*), also designed by Piano in 1992, is one of the largest in Europe (much visited by school parties), with 50 huge tanks that can be viewed both from an underwater level and from above. The natural habitat of the Red Sea and the Caribbean coral reef have been reconstructed; and you can admire some 20,000 creatures, including dolphins, seals and sharks, and tropical fish.

MuMA

The Galata Museo del Mare, the Commenda di San Giovanni di Prè and the Museo Navale di Pegli make up a singular 'distributed museum', MuMA (Musei del Mare e della Migrazione), whose mission is to increase awareness of the sea as a means of communication and to enhance dialogue between populations and cultures.

Galata Museo del Mare: *Map Genoa West, 1; Calata De Mari 1 / Metro Darsena. Open March–Oct, daily 10–7.30; Nov–Feb Tues–Fri 10–6, Sat, Sun and holidays 10–7.30; www.galatamuseodelmare.it.* This large and fascinating museum of the Mediterranean (10,000 m2) occupies 23 rooms on four floors in a contemporary stone-and-glass building designed by Seville architect Guillermo Vázquez Consuegra. It traces the history of the port of Genoa, skilfully combining 'hard' exhibits with interactive and multimedia supports. Highlights include a reconstructed 17th-century Genoese galley and a 19th-century brigantine (inside the museum) and a modern submarine (the *Nazario Sauro*, constructed in 1976, decommissioned in 2002) moored outside; other open-air exhibits include what may be the world's only collection of historic harbour cranes. There are rooms dedicated to eminent Genoese mariners (notably Christopher Columbus), an arsenal, an armoury, and a (very effective) virtual-reality Cape Horn tempest. The top floor is devoted to immigration: historic Italian emigration to the New World (with a focus on the United States, Argentina and Brazil; you can pilot your own steamship) and contemporary immigration to Italy, largely from Africa. At the very top is a sunny panoramic terrace.

Museoteatro della Commenda di Prè: *Map Genoa West, 1; Piazza della Commenda / Metro Principe. Open Tues–Fri 10–5; Sat, Sun and holidays 10–7.* At the north end of the old harbour, the church of San Giovanni di Prè, founded in 1180, adjoins the Commenda, the Commandery of the Knights Hospitaller of St John, built at the same time as a convent and hospice for crusaders. On Piazza Commenda you can see the fine five-spired campanile and flank of the church, with its Gothic windows, next to the beautiful triple loggia of the Commenda, altered in the Renaissance. In the latest of a long series of restorations and role changes, the complex has recently (2009) been dressed out as a 'theatre-museum' where sophisticated technologies bring significant historical events and their leading figures to life. The exhibits, some a bit melodramatic, underscore the historical importance of Genoa as an international crossroads and of the Knights of St John as cultural mediators. The museum has a rich events programme, tailored to recall the Commandery's historic role as a place of hospitality for pilgrims and travellers.

The Museo Navale is described in the paragraphs devoted to the museums of Pegli.

PASSEGGIATA ALLA LANTERNA AND MUSEO DELLA LANTERNA

The **Passeggiata alla Lanterna**, or Lighthouse Promenade, is a new pedestrian path connecting the old harbour to the Lanterna (*beyond map Genoa West, 1*), Genoa's lighthouse, long a symbol of the city. The promenade, which enables walkers to reach the lighthouse from the ferry terminal (*starting point: Via Milano, between the ferry terminal shopping centre car park and the Columbus Sea Hotel; Metro Dinegro*) in just 10mins without touching on the bustling dock area, is a continuation of Genoa's ancient access route from the west, called the Tagliata della Lanterna because it was partly hewn (*tagliata*) from the rock. Text panels along the way provide notes on what went on at the docks over the centuries. The walkway is 800m long and develops in level and stepped tracts in galvanised steel and wood, crossing over the 17th-century walls and the later Savoy fortifications. There is a tree-shaded rest area halfway along, and a little park at the foot of the Lanterna itself.

The latter is still Genoa's lighthouse, but it's automatic now, which has freed up its base for other uses. The edifice you see today dates from 1543 and replaces a 12th-century lighthouse that was destroyed in 1514. Domenico Chiodo designed the New Lantern Gate and its fortifications for Carlo Alberto of Savoy in 1827, and these, together with the lighthouse proper, are now the site of the **Museo della Lanterna** (*open Sat, Sun and holidays 10–7*), where multimedia exhibits making extensive use of videos and holograms present local history and ethnography. There is also a section on lighthouses and their intriguing mechanisms.

THE PEGLI MUSEUMS

Pegli (*map A, D2*) is an upmarket residential neighbourhood located on Genoa's western outskirts. Once a renowned health resort, is is the only district west of Genoa that has not suffered the consequences of industrialisation and has managed, at least in part, to remain a tourist destination. It retains the appearance of an old-fashioned fishing village and thanks to its mild climate and its parks, villas and two excellent museums—the Museo Navale di Pegli and Museo di Archeologia Ligure—it is still considered one of the most beautiful and characteristic parts of the city. The name is a corruption of *Pyla Veituriorum*, the village established here by the Ligurian tribe of the Veturii. It was the birthplace of Pope Benedict XV (Giacomo della Chiesa) and of singer-songwriter Fabrizio De André.

Getting there

There are three ways to get to Pegli from central Genoa: the fastest is by rail (c. 15mins from Piazza Principe Station; map Genoa West, 1); the most nerve-racking is by bus (no. 1 or 3 from Piazza Di Negro; just beyond map Genoa West, 1) and the most scenic is by boat (Navebus, from Piazza Caricamento, map Genoa West, 6, in c. 30mins). In fair weather this is far and away the best way to go.

The ancient fishing village extends along the seashore for more than two kilometres. The **Lungomare di Pegli** is overlooked by a string of lovely old buildings unbroken by new construction and surrounded by fishermen's houses, medieval ruins and 19th-century townhouses. The **old town** extends from the area around the central Piazza Porticciolo to Via Carloforte, the *caruggio* that leads to the so-called Palace of the Pope, birthplace of Benedict XV. The hills above are sprinkled with Art Nouveau villas built as suburban homes or summer houses. The Pegli museums occupy two grand old villas, one next to the other.

The **Museo Navale di Pegli**, in the 16th-century Renaissance villa of Giovanni Andrea Doria (*Piazza Bonavino 7; open Tues–Fri 9–1, Sat 10–6, Sun and holidays 10–1*) tells the maritime history Genoa and, particularly, its rivieras from the 15th–19th centuries, through maps, paintings, drawings, ship models, nautical instruments and reconstructions of old shipyards and artisans' workshops. Here you'll discover that the beaches that are now the main 'merchandise' of Liguria's flourishing tourist trade were once one great, open-air arsenal – for it is here that the region's great merchant and naval fleets were physically assembled. There are some very finely crafted models in the stuccoed and frescoed rooms, and an excellent collection of the material culture of Ligurian mariners and shipwrights.

The recently renovated **Museo di Archeologia Ligure**, in the nearby Villa Pallavicini (*Via Pallavicini 11; open Tues–Fri 9–7, Sat, Sun and holidays 10–7*), has beautiful displays of regional prehistoric and protohistoric finds, including some remarkable material from the palaeolithic tombs of the Arene Candide cave (the oldest, called the *Tomba del Principe* by virtue of its extraordinarily rich treasure, dates from more than 23,000 years ago). There are also numerous items from Genoa's pre-Roman necropolis (among them the *Tavola di Polcevera*, the oldest Roman inscription in the region, 117 BC), and from Roman towns in the region. Special sections are devoted to the Greek and Roman collections of Prince Odone of Savoy, to Egyptian antiquities (notably the Pasherienaset mummy and its sarcophagus), Roman marbles, and to the great bears that wintered in the region's caves during the last glaciation, some 80,000 years ago.

The villa and its park were designed for Ignazio Alessandro Pallavicini by Michele Canzo (the brother of Stefano, architect of the Teatro Carlo Felice) and built in the 1840s. The park, now a **botanical garden** run by the University of Genoa, is above all one of the finest Romantic gardens in Italy and merits a visit in its own right. The architect has created an ingenious series of 'stage sets' that form a fascinating walk-through 'opera' in three acts plus prologue and epilogue. Broad, shady paths lead past Neoclassical, Gothic Revival and faux-rustic architectural creations, through delightful grottoes, over bridges and past brilliant white sculptures by the Genoese

Giovanni Battista Cevasco, to the Great Lake, a metaphor of Paradise. There are native evergreen oaks and laurels, plus a number of exotics, including palms, camphor and camellia trees.

MODERN GENOA

PIAZZA DELLA VITTORIA

The spacious level area outside the city walls called *il Prato* (the Meadow), where Piazza della Vittoria (*map Genoa East, 16*) and Piazza Verdi (*Metro Brignole*) are now situated, was used in the 16th century for archery practice and until the 19th century as a parade ground. Originally the alluvial basin of the Bisagno torrent, nestled between the hill of the historic city centre and that of Albaro, where well-to-do Genoese built their summer houses, in 1873 the area was turned into a city park. The first ideas for a comprehensive redesign were put forward at the end of the 19th century, when Via XX Settembre and Brignole Station were built.

In 1923 the city council announced a tender for a garden endowed with arena, stadium or open-air theatre, swimming-pool and war memorial in Piazza Verdi and Piazza di Francia, the present Piazza della Vittoria. The tender was won by the most prominent Italian architect of the day, Marcello Piacentini, but in 1924 another tender was called by the *Corriere Mercantile*, an important city newspaper, to mark its first centenary. The new competition called for the interment of the Bisagno (unthinkable in today's environmentally-conscious world and fiercely punished by flash floods in 1945, 1951, 1992 and 2011), a move intended to pave the way (literally) for the construction of the modern quarter now known as La Foce. The tender was again won by Piacentini, together with the sculptor Arturo Dazzi, who designed the square's war memorial-cum-triumphal arch (1927–1931). Local residents did not appreciate the project at the time (Piacentini and Dazzi were both close to the Fascist regime, whereas Genoa was notoriously anti-Fascist), and in 1928 the town council accepted a series of changes suggested by the other architects who had participated in the second competition. It was decided to turn Piazza Verdi into gardens and to erect six buildings on Piazza di Francia with more gardens at the centre and a large public building on the seaward side. The monumental character of the buildings, the surrounding colonnade, the setback of the fronts of the central buildings, and the use of fine materials, including external stone cladding, were all specified in the competition and remained unchanged. The interment of the Bisagno began in 1928, and in 1932 two smaller buildings (the present Liceo Andrea Doria and Questura) were added on the seaward side of the square with a green area in the middle rising up the knoll of Carignano. Piacentini was assisted by the architects Paolo Fossati and Beniamino Bellati. Alfredo Fineschi designed the Carignano stepped garden.

PIAZZA DANTE

When Greater Genoa was formed in 1926, linking 19 neighbouring municipalities from Voltri to Nervi, the city government decided to give a striking new design to the town's economic centre, which had shifted from the Banchi area, in the heart of the historic centre, to Piazza De Ferrari and Piazza Dante (*map Genoa East, 11*). The area was already heavily built up, but in the heyday of the Modernist 'urban renewal', revitalising it meant ripping out the pre-existing urban fabric and building something shiny and new in its place. As had the creation of Piazza De Ferrari and Via XX Settembre in 1887 and 1897, so too did the construction in the 1930s of the present piazza Dante take a high toll on historic architecture. Architects Aldo Viale and Giulio Zappa won the competition for the area's new design in 1933. Their plan included four buildings that exceeded the maximum height allowed by the then-current building regulations. In 1937 the town council approved a variation of the plan, which reduced the number of those buildings from four to two, and in 1938 an ancillary plan was approved for the restoration of Porta Soprana, one of the gates in the 12th-century city walls, which included the demolition of the surrounding buildings.

Thus Piazza Dante was created, between 1935 and 1940, by knocking down the historic Ponticello and Morcento districts. The first tall building to be built was Giuseppe Rosso's 1937 **Grattacielo Nord**, a U-shaped tower c. 80m high with commercial space on the lower floors and residential space above. Its most distinctive feature is the setback of the tower windows from the façade, meant to protect them from Genoa's notoriously strong winds. The second and last tall building was Marcello Piacentini's **Grattacielo Sud**, a 120m 'clocktower skyscraper' intended as an all-Italian version of the American prototype. It consists of a porticoed base embellished by Guido Galletti's bas-reliefs of Christopher Columbus and 'Balilla' (Giovan Battista Perasso, the child patriot who threw the first stone against the occupying Austrian troops at Porta Soprana, sparking the revolt of 1746) and a 23-storey tower, which tapers off at the top to form steps like the skyscrapers of New York or Chicago. Alternate bands of brick and stone notionally link the tower walls to those of Genoa's churches and patrician palaces. Mosaics by Oscar Saccorotti and Lorenzo Martinelli decorate the ground-floor cinema-theatre, and the penthouse holds a restaurant with a panoramic terrace, originally owned and managed by Martini. In 1966 a new office district was built in the former Borghi Lanaioli and Marina districts, completing the urban renewal projects begun in the Fascist period and blocking the view from Piazza Dante to the sea.

From Piazza Danta Via Fieschi ascends to the red and white classical church of **Santa Maria Assunta di Carignano** (*map Genoa East, 15*), one of the best works of Galeazzo Alessi (begun in 1552). The sculptures on the façade are by Claude David, and inside on the dome piers are statues (1662–90) by Pierre Puget, Filippo Parodi and Claude David. Via Nino Bixio and Via Ruffini lead southeast from here to Villa Croce, the cultural hub of modern Genoa.

MUSEO D'ARTE CONTEMPORANEA VILLA CROCE
Via J. Ruffini 3 (beyond map Genoa East, 15). Open Tues–Fri 9–1, Sat 10–1; exhibitions Tues–Fri 9–6.30, Sat, Sun and holidays 10–6.30.
The collections here include more than 3,000 works of Italian and foreign abstract

art, the best of which are from the Maria Cernuschi Ghiringhelli collection, comprising more than 200 works by leading Italian and international artists. Among those represented are Josef Albers (1888–1976), Sonia Delaunay (1885–1979), Jasper Johns (1930–), Piero Manzoni (1933–1963), Mimmo Rotella (1918–2006) and Jesus Raphael Soto (1923–2005), as well as Italian artists who are well known at home but less famous abroad. The Neoclassical villa and its park enjoy splendid views, over the waterfront Fiera di Genova (home to the world-famous Genoa Boat Show in October) to the sea.

ALBARO, BOCCADASSE & QUARTO

On the wooded hill to the east of the centre, the **Albaro** neighbourhood holds some of the city's finest suburban villas. At Via Albaro 4, **Villa Saluzzo Bombrini**, also known as Il Paradiso for its beautiful garden, was built by Vannone for Giacomo Saluzzo in the 16th century. Now owned by FAI (Fondo Italiano per l'Ambiente) and opened to the public for special events, it was the home of singer-songwriter Fabrizio De André (1940–99). Gino Paoli (1934–), another well-known singer-songwriter, lives in the *dépendence*. Across the street is **Villa Saluzzo Mongiardino**, where Byron lived in 1822. The university faculty of engineering occupies the splendid **Villa Giustiniani Cambiaso** (*Via Montallegro I*), built in 1548 on a design by Galeazzo Alessi, with another garden. In Via San Nazaro, the **Villa Bagnerello** (plaque) was where Dickens lived in 1844 before moving into central Genoa: 'I was set down in a rank, dull, weedy courtyard, attached to a kind of pink jail; and was told I lived there.'

A casual stroll will take you by all these places in less than half an hour. Walking another 30mins through the wooded streets will take you to the tiny old fishing port of **Boccadasse**, still very well preserved. It has good fish restaurants and a popular ice-cream shop. A half-hour further east is **Quarto**, where a monument marks the starting-point of Garibaldi and the 'Thousand' (*'I Mille'*) on their expedition to Sicily (5th May 1860). The expedition was the first major campaign in the five-year war that united the many city-states of Italy under the rule of a single king, Vittorio Emanuele of Savoy. Villa Spinola, where Garibaldi stayed while planning the expedition with his friend Candido Augusto Vecchi, hosts a small Museo Garibaldino (*open Tues–Sun 3–6*).

NERVI & ITS MUSEUMS

Nervi (*map B, A2*), Genoa's beautiful garden suburb, marks the beginning of the Riviera di Levante, the eastern riviera, made especially luxuriant by the rain that falls when the moist sea breezes encounter the high mountains of the shore. Between Genoa and the Portofino Peninsula extends a broad bay so verdant it is known as the Golfo del Paradiso. As early as the 16th century this became a favourite spot for the construction of villas and gardens. Four of these former country houses and their parks have recently been combined to form a magnificent centre of fine arts, architecture and garden design, the **Parchi e Musei di Nervi**. Three of the four parks, though criss-crossed by the Genoa–Rome rail line and some minor roads connecting the main Via Aurelia to the waterfront, form a single, large green space with some outstanding plants and marvellous sea views. The fourth (the villa and park of the Museo Giannettino Luxoro) is set apart from the rest by a few properties that are still in private hands. All four can be reached by the Via Aurelia (now the main street of old Nervi) or from the lovely Passeggiata Anita Garibaldi, a two-kilometre long paved walkway built right on the rocks and enjoying magnificent sea views. Nervi's little *borgo marinaro* has been a destination for Sunday strolls since the 19th century.

Getting to Nervi

The Nervi Parks and Museums are located a few dozen metres east of Nervi railway station: exit the station and turn immediately left, passing beneath the tracks to the Passeggiata Anita Garibaldi. Turn left again and follow the signs or the inscribed bricks in the pavement, to the museums. The station is served by treni regionali and interegionali between Genoa and Sestri Levante/La Spezia, and by the Voltri–Nervi Metro light rail line. You can also take AMT bus lines 15, 17 and 517 eastbound from Piazza De Ferrari, via Dante or Brignole Station: the 15 and 17 will leave you at Nervi borgo, where you pick up the 517 for Capolungo (Galleria d'Arte Moderna stop), or walk the 200m or so to the first museums.

MUSEO GIANNETTINO LUXORO

Villa Luxoro, Viale Mafalda di Savoia 3. Open Tues–Fri 9–1; Sat 10–1.

This early 20th-century house holds collections of paintings and drawings, furniture and decorative arts from the 18th and 19th centuries, bequeathed to the city by the heirs of Giannettino Luxoro, who died in the First World War. The villa, which once stood amidst olive and citrus groves, was designed specifically to exhibit the family collection. Its form and decoration imitates those of Genoese architecture of earlier centuries, and its original appearance and atmosphere have been preserved throughout.

The most important single body of works displayed here is probably the **clock collection**, which includes some 50 timepieces ranging in date from the 17th to the 19th century. The most entertaining is undoubtedly the collection of **Christmas crêche figurines**, dating from the 17th and 18th centuries. The finely dressed wooden figures, and the horses and other animals, are exquisitely rendered. Highlights here are a set of unclothed figures in wood, and a magnificent set of painted paper figures, from the 18th century. The **decorative arts collections** include Ligurian majolicas, a Savona tea set with its distinctive figures and ruins, Chinese porcelain, and ceramics from Faenza and other Italian centres. The furniture collection is particularly unusual, as most pieces were made locally in the 18th century. For reasons of conservation, the museum's collection of 16th–19th-century fabrics is shown in temporary exhibitions only.

The **park** follows an unpretentious modern design featuring native Mediterranean trees and shrubs: evergreen oaks, umbrella pines, cypresses, Aleppo pines and carob trees; mastic (*Pistacia lentiscus*), strawberry trees (*Arbutus unedo*) and other components of the community of evergreen shrubs and small trees typical of Mediterranean coastal regions, the *macchia mediterranea* or *maquis*.

RACCOLTE FRUGONE

Villa Grimaldi Fassio, Via Capolungo 9. Open Tues–Fri 9–7, Sat, Sun and holidays 10–7.

The 18th-century Villa Grimaldi Fassio holds the collections of the brothers Lazzaro and Luigi Frugone. Here are paintings, sculptures, drawings and engravings—mainly portraits, genre scenes and landscapes, in keeping with the tastes of upper-class collectors of the early 20th century—ranging in date from the 1860s to the 1930s. Among the many things you're unlikely to see elsewhere are paintings by the Belle Époque nonconformist painters known as the *Scapigliati* (the 'Unkempt'); a beautiful, large portrait by society painter Giovanni Boldini (*Miss Bell*); an intimate family portrait by post-Impressionist Giuseppe De Nittis (*L'Amaca*), and some very fine paintings by the Tuscan Macchiaioli artists Giovanni Fattori (*Buoi in riva all'Arno* and *Pattuglia di cavalleggeri*) and Telemaco Signorini (*Vegetazione a Riomaggiore*, a gorgeous little painting of the Cinque Terre). Not to be missed is the drawing collection, on the top floor, kept in drawers that are opened one by one, by museum staff.

The east end of the park of the Villa Grimaldi Fassio holds an internationally renowned **rose garden** restored in 2012 and renamed after its founder, Luigi Viacava. It features c. 300 varieties of roses.

GALLERIA D'ARTE MODERNA

Villa Saluzzo Serra, Via Capolungo 3. Open Tues–Sun 10–6.

This sumptuous villa, built in the late 16th century for Agostino Romeo, was sold in 1611 to Bartolomeo Saluzzo and then again in the early 19th century to the Serra marquises, who were probably responsible for most of the interior decoration and for the Romantic garden. It was acquired by the city of Genoa in the 1920s and has housed the Modern Art Gallery ever since. Originally comprising the core of the collection of Prince Odone di Savoia and subsequently augmented with donations and acquisitions, the **gallery** preserves more than 2,700 paintings, sculptures, drawings and engravings from the early 19th century to the present. The best known of the artists displayed are Felice Casorati (1883–1963), Primo Conti (1900–88), Fortunato Depero (1892–1960), Filippo De Pisis (1896–1956), Renato Guttuso (1911–87), Mario Mafai (1902–65) and Arturo Martini (1889–1947). The most distinctive works, however, belong to an earlier period. These are the 19th-century landscape paintings of the Scuola dei Grigi, a circle of friends which grew up in Liguria between 1860 and 1880 and advocated a new approach to Northern Italian landscape painting inspired by the naturalism then in vogue in France. The most celebrated *Grigio* was Ernesto Rayper; the theorist of the movement, Tammar Luxoro. Their works are placed in context amidst those of other Naturalist painters, such as the Macchiaioli Vincenzo Cabianca and Luigi Bechi, and the view painters Gerolamo and Domenico Induno, Massimo D'Azeglio, Francesco Inganni and Domenico Morelli. Other memorable works include the large painting of labourers in a shipyard by the Divisionist Plinio Nomellini, and an absolutely magnificent room of furniture designed by visual artist Duilio Cambellotti for the Palazzo dell'Acquedotto Pugliese in Bari; Cambellotti drew his inspiration from William Morris, with whom he shared a belief in the social and ethical value of art.

In the Romantic **park** is the Serra family chapel, with a fine slate and marble floor and a polychrome marble balustrade and altar; the altarpiece with the *Madonna and Child with Saints*, is by an anonymous 18th-century Ligurian artist. By the entrance to the restored stables are two very rare Chilean wine palms (*Jubaea chilensis*). This is the only species in the genus *Jubaea* in the palm family *Arecaceae*; it is native to a small area of central Chile, and the two examples you see here are among the finest in the world. Other exotics include camellia trees (*Camellia japonica*) cedars and thujas; among the native trees are the lovely tall cypresses, umbrella pines, evergreen oaks, some beautiful old olives and the ever-present laurel. The museum café serves refreshments, in full view of a large and popular playground.

WOLFSONIANA

Villa Serra Gropallo, Via Serra Gropallo, 4. Open Wed–Sun 10–6, www.wolfsoniana.it. Unique among the collections of the Nervi museums in that the collector is still very much alive and active, the Wolfsoniana focuses on decorative and propaganda art from the 1880s to the mid-20th century. Here you'll find paintings, sculptures, graphic arts, furniture, everyday items and objects of industrial design representing all the major movements from late 19th-century Exoticism to Art Nouveau, the Novecento, Art Deco and Rationalism. Particularly interesting is the silver produced by the Ligurian artisan Arrigo Finzi on the basis of designs by the architect Antonio Sant'Elia. Sant'Elia was a brilliant Futurist, a native of Como, whose work is only known (apart from a single villa above Como) from his writings and drawings, particularly those for an imagined *Città Nuova*: he was killed in the First World War, aged 28. The 1919 Futurist centrepiece displayed here is based on Sant-Elia's sketches, though it was produced posthumously. Later, in the 1930s, Finzi registered a Sant'Elia trademark, but the silverware made under this name represents a revision of the Futurist architect's ideas in the light of more current fashions, notably Art Deco.

Another highlight of the collection is the children's room designed entirely by Silvio Spaventa Filippi, journalist, graphic designer and founder of *Corriere dei Piccoli*, the children's supplement to *Corriere della Sera*, published from 1908 until 1995.

The Wolfsoniana's collection of 20th-century Italian propaganda art is stunning (in every way), and the temporary exhibitions are always extremely well conceived and displayed.

PASSEGGIATA ANITA GARIBALDI

This seaside promenade stretches from the little harbour of Nervi to that of

Capolungo, some 2km southeast. Named after Anita, wife of Giuseppe Garibaldi and a patriot in her own right, it follows an ancient path used by local fishermen and farmers, offering magnificent views (and the added thrill of stormy seas in winter) across the Golfo del Paradiso to the Portofino Peninsula.

The **Porticiolo**, Nervi's little harbour, was constructed on a bay at the turn of the 19th century. Packed with fishing boats and surrounded by pastel-coloured houses, it is a picturesque place with a tiny beach, a public pool, and a number of cafés and restaurants that become crowded and lively on summer evenings.

Capolungo, also called Sant'Ilario al Mare, is the most easterly neighbourhood in the Genoa municipality; it was a resort until the mid-20th century, when most of its grand hotels were converted into flats. The Marina di Capolungo, like the Porticiolo di Nervi, is a picturesque little fishing port.

The main village of **Sant'Ilario**, set amidst citrus groves and mimosas c. 200m above sea level, has a very pretty church founded in the 11th century but modified several times since. It is reached by Via alla Chiesa di Sant'Ilario, a steep *creusa* (or paved walkway; same root as *caruggio*) starting from the Via Aurelia at Capolungo and enjoys breathtaking views. The actor Rudolph Valentino (Rodolfo Alfonso Pietro Filiberto Raffaello Guglielmi, 1895–1926) obtained a degree in agriculture at the Istituto Professionale Marsano here before emigrating to America.

PRACTICAL TIPS

GETTING AROUND

City buses, Metro trains, funiculars and short-haul ferries are run by AMT (*www.amt.genova.it*). Single-journey tickets valid for 100mins in the metropolitan area can be purchased at newsstands and tobacconists, AMT and railway ticket offices. A ticket valid for one day on any line can be purchased as above, or online. Taxis are independently operated and can be hired at taxi stands or by phone, T: 010 5966.

WHERE TO STAY IN GENOA

€€ **Hotel Bristol Palace.** This elegant Art Nouveau building on Genoa's grandest street has many famous names in its guest book, including Luigi Pirandello, Gabriele D'Annunzio, Emperor Hirohito and Alfred Hitchcock. Hitchcock is said to have taken the elliptical staircase as his inspiration when designing the swirling staircases of *Vertigo*. Whether or not it is true matters little: the breathtaking staircase is just one component of the hotel's painstakingly restored interior, which preserves most of its original structure and furnishings. Even the antique beds and armoires are genuine. *Via XX Settembre 35, T: 010 592541, www. hotelbristolpalace.it. Map Genoa East, 11.*

€€ **Villa Pagoda.** This is an extraordinary place, offering great comfort in a 19th-century villa with gardens, just a short walk from the sea. The best of Genoa as it once was, and ideally located for visiting the parks and museums of Nervi. *Via Capolungo 15 (at Nervi). T: 010 372 6161, www. villapagoda.it.*

€ **Locanda di Palazzo Cicala.** A place of great charm in the heart of old Genoa, this inn occupies the main floor of a beautifully restored 17th-century palace opposite the cathedral of San Lorenzo. Just a ten-minute walk from the old harbour and Piazza De Ferrari. In days of old, important visitors to Genoa were hosted by the city's great families in their sumptuous homes, *the rolli* and a stay here offers an opportunity to relive that experience. Behind a Rococo façade the ground-floor entrance and its staircase abound in arches and columns, and several of the contemporary-furnished rooms are decorated with stuccoes or frescoes. Children are welcome, and a babysitter is available on request. *Piazza San Lorenzo 16, T: 010 251 8824, www. palazzocicala.it. Map Genoa West, 10.*

WHERE TO EAT IN GENOA

€€ **Antica Osteria del Bai.** In 1804 Pope Pius VII stopped in this tavern by the water (est.1790) while on his way to Paris to crown Napoleon, and in 1860 Garibaldi had a last drink here before embarking for Sicily with the Thousand. Located in a former watchtower whose thick stone walls offer excellent insulation from the summer heat, the little *osteria* used to be known for the twin pine trees growing on its roof; today it is a refined restaurant whose reputation is due to its exquisite cuisine, an interesting balance between tradition and imagination. Closed Mon. *Via Quarto 12, at Quarto, 5km east of the centre; T: 010 387478, www.osteriadelbai.it.*

€€ **La Berlocca.** This very simple establishment serves up great regional dishes, with a special focus on pastas, vegetables and seafood. It's convenient if you're visiting the city centre, being just around the corner from the Strada Nuova. *Via dei Macelli di Soziglia 45r, T: 010 247 4162, www.laberlocca.com. Map Genoa East, 7.*

€€ **Pansön.** This old family restaurant (mainly pasta and fish) in the peaceful Piazza delle Erbe has been in business since 1790. Nelson reputedly ate here and the little back room is named in his honour. The cooking here is reliable, not fancy. Closed Sun. *Piazza delle Erbe 5. T: 010 2468903, www. ristorantepanson.com. Map Genoa East, 11.*

€€ **Da Rina.** This family-run trattoria by the old harbour is famous for its seafood dishes; some would say they're the best in town. They don't come cheap, but the quality/price ratio is high, and Rina enjoys a strong local following. *Mura delle Grazie 3R (just east of Piazza delle Grazie; map Genoa West, 10), T: 010 246 6475, www. ristorantedarina.it.*

€€ **Taverna detta del Bruxaboschi.** The Risorgimento was conceived in Turin and planned in Genoa. But where, exactly? It's a 20min taxi drive from Piazza De Ferrari to the old village of San Desiderio, in the hills above Quarto, where Giuseppe

Mazzini and the *Giovine Italia* group of republican revolutionaries met secretly in the early 1830s. This was the only tavern in the village at the time, which makes it reasonable to presume they spent a good deal of their time here, far from indiscreet glances—and, of course, from the police. Admittedly 20mins is a long drive just to dine with the ghost of Mazzini, but the patriot is the pretext, not the reason, for coming here—as any of the *genovesi* who make the trek here (especially at weekends) will tell. *Via F. Mignone 8, at San Desiderio, T: 010 3450302, www. bruxaboschi.com.*

€€ Trattoria Rosmarino. Well-liked place in the heart of town, right behind the Palazzo Ducale. Local seasonal cooking and a competent, modern atmosphere. Closed Sun. *Salita del Fondaco 30. T: 010 2510475, www. trattoriarosmarino.it. Map Genoa East, 11.*

€–€€ M Café. You will see a number of café-restaurants in this chain around the city, including in Palazzo Rosso, Palazzo Ducale and Palazzo Reale. The aim, by their own admission, is to create an 'informal, convivial and creative atmoshphere' in museums and historic palaces. The formula is good value, easy and relaxed. Go there just for coffee and a croissant, for a snack, an aperitif or lunch/brunch. *www.m-cafe.it.*

€ Caffè Pasticceria Mangini. Half a century ago this excellent café and pastry shop would have been crowded with loud, smoke-puffing journalists from Genoa's two daily newspapers, *Il Secolo XIX* and *Il Lavoro*, both of which were located nearby. *Il Lavoro* closed in the 1990s and *Il Secolo XIX* has since moved, so things are a bit quieter today,

though Mangini is still a place where the city's professional class gathers. The coffee is reputedly the best in town, and the antique furnishings, with abundant wood and crystal, create an atmosphere of sober elegance. *Piazza Corvetto 3R, T: 010 56401013. Map Genoa East, 8.*

€ Confettieri Pietro Romanengo fu Stefano. Italy's most famous confectioner 'exquisitely candied all manner of fruits', Giuseppe Verdi wrote. King Umberto of Savoy chose Romanengo to cater his wedding to Queen Margherita; the city of Savona presented Romanengo *demizuccheri* to Vittorio Emanuele II when he visited there in 1857, and singer-songwriter Fabrizio De André immortalised the establishment in song. The candied fruits, fruit and flower preserves (the rose sugar and rose syrup are famous), fondants, bonbons, chocolates and dragées are all made from historic recipes, for which the shop's rich exterior and interior décor is a perfect match. *Via Soziglia 74/76R, map Genoa East, 7. Also at Via Roma 51R, www. romanengo.it. Map Genoa East, 7.*

€ Pasticceria Liquoreria Marescotti Cavo. If you were wondering where Stendhal bought the Morello-cherry liqueur of which he was so fond, now you know. Established in 1750 in an ancient alley near the steamship docks, the Marescotti pastry and liqueur shop has long been a favourite of travellers. After it closed in 1979, following the death of the last of the Marescotti dynasty of *pasticcieri*, it was purchased and restored by another well-known family of pastry makers, the Cavo, who reopened it in 2008. The poplar, maple and rosewood cabinetry is superb, and Rubens is said to have designed the floor, for a palace on the Strada Nuova. By all standards the most exquisite things here, however, are edible. *Via di Fossatello 35R and 37R, between Piazza Fossatello and Via San Luca, map Genoa West, 6. T: 010 2091226, www. cavo.it.*

€ Pasticceria Svizzera Vital Gaspero. Very Swiss. This establishment of 1910, with its pristine white interior coloured only by a small Swiss cross high up on the wall, is a masterpiece of quiet stylishness. Swiss pastry shops took Genoa by storm in the late 19th and early 20th centuries, offering fragrances and flavours from the Germanic tradition and becoming so fashionable as to threaten the very existence of rivals offering only local fare. Now this is the only one left, and it seems destined to last, its clientèle coming largely from the wealthy Albaro neighbourhood. *Via Albaro 9R, beyond map Genoa East, 16. T: 010 3629278, www.pasticceriasvizzera.it.*

Genoa is the home of ***focaccia***, the delicious soft, low white bread that goes well with just about anything. You can buy *focaccia* in most bakeries and grocery shops—plain (have it sliced open and stuffed with cold meats, cheeses, sun-dried tomatoes, olive spread, etc. for a truly memorable sandwich) or topped with cheese, onions or potatoes. Equally good but less well known is ***farinata***, a type of pizza-sized pancake made with chick-pea flour, extra virgin olive oil, water and salt. A popular food from Nice to Pisa, in Genoa it is sold in modest snack bars called *farinotti*. These include Sa Pesta (*Via dei Giustiniani 16, map Genoa West, 10–11*) and Sciamadda (*Via Ravecca 19, map Genoa East, 11*).

The Riviera di Ponente

Today the resident population of Liguria is extremely dense and is increased by some three million annual visitors, roughly a third of whom are foreigners. Most of the population is concentrated along the coast, which appears, especially at night when the city lights sparkle in the terse air, as a single, ribbon-like metropolis with Genoa at its centre. Transport links hug the coast too. Both the railway and the Via Aurelia (SS1) stick close to the sea. The extension of the Via Aurelia, the Roman Via Julia Augusta, was built by the emperor Augustus to carry traffic across the Alps to Gaul two millennia ago. The SS1 still presents a viable alternative to the *autostrada*, which can be very busy in summer or on sunny weekends. That the rivieras are just an hour and a half by car from Milan and Turin make short getaways popular: bear this in mind if you visit the region by car. Traffic on the *autostrada* can come to a complete standstill on Friday and Sunday evenings, as well as Saturday mornings when towns have their outdoor markets

The Riviera del Ponente, literally the 'Sunset Riviera', is the section of coast stretching westwards from Genoa towards France. Its resorts mostly follow a common plan: an old town on the hillside with steep, narrow streets (*caruggi* in Ligurian dialect, *creuze* when in the countryside) and houses that may date as far back as the 13th or 14th century; a new town on the coast with attractive villas and hotels, gardens and scenic promenades; and a small seaport, occasionally overlooked by a Genoese fort. If you enjoy gardening, you will want to linger along the Riviera dei Fiori, the segment nearest France. Ventimiglia has a stunning botanical garden established by two Englishmen (Giardini Botanici Hanbury); the Institute of Ligurian Studies in Bordighera displays a unique collection of Mediterranean flora; San Remo has the most important flower market in Italy; and all through the hills flowers can be seen being grown in hothouses. Almost all the towns have interesting historic centres: an example is Albenga, with its fine old cathedral and mosaic-lined baptistery, the lovely little Piazzetta dei Leoni, home to three proud Renaissance lions, and the bishops' palace with its frescoed façade. Throughout the region one can walk in famous footsteps: Tchaikovsky finished his *Fourth Symphony* and *Eugene Onegin* in San Remo, and D.H. Lawrence wrote *Lady Chatterley's Lover* amidst the cascading bougainvillea of Sportorno. There is also a strong tradition of food and wine, made manifest in institutions such as the Museo dell'Olivo in Oneglia, devoted to olive oil, its production and uses (*www.museodellolivo.com*), and in the Riviera's many excellent restaurants.

THE RIVIERA DEI FIORI

Many years ago some marketing genius (or geniuses) divided the Riviera di Ponente into two segments: the Riviera dei Fiori, extending from the French border to Andora, and the Riviera delle Palme, from Andora to Varazze. If historical accuracy, rather than hotel occupancy, were the determining criterion, the Riviera dei Fiori would be called the *Riviera degli Agrumeti*, for it was the citrus groves here that most impressed the earliest visitors to this coast: the hothouses with their flowers came much, much later. Western Liguria was—and is—also one of the leading olive-oil regions of the Mediterranean, and the coastal plain has always produced delicious vegetables. The area around San Bartolomeo al Mare, for example, is known for its astonishingly tender artichokes. In the alluvial basin of the River Impero the main crop was hemp, used to make the sails and rigging of Genoese merchant vessels and warships.

VENTIMIGLIA AND THE BORDERLANDS

One expects every frontier town to have a split personality, but Ventimiglia's (*map A, A2*) is topographical rather than cultural. It is Menton, in France, that looks and feels Italian while being French; in Ventimiglia, France could just as well be on the other side of the globe. The split here is created by the River Roia, which divides the urban fabric quite abruptly into an old medieval town on a hill to the west and a new town on the coastal plain between the railway and the Via Aurelia.

The old town is pleasant but not pretty. Its most important monument is the 11th–12th-century **cathedral**, a handsome stone edifice with a portal of 1222 and a barrel-vaulted nave; its apse adjoins the 11th-century baptistery, equally dignified and, perhaps because of its scale, somewhat less austere. In **San Michele**, rebuilt c. 1100, the stoups are made from Roman milestones, and the Romanesque crypt is perfectly preserved. Work is underway to transform the central **Piazza Borea** into a public park, with shade trees and aromatic Mediterranean plants. The Forte dell'Annunziata, on Via Verdi, at the edge of the old town, houses the small but interesting **Museo Archeologico Girolamo Rossi** (*open winter Tues–Sat 9–12.30 & 3–5, Sun and holidays 10–12.30; summer Tues–Thur 9–12.30 & 3–5, Fri 9–11pm, Sat 9–12.30, Sun 9–11pm; www.fortedellannunziata.it/iL_museo.htm*); founded in 1900 by Sir Thomas Hanbury, it contains finds from the Roman *Albintimilium*, where Agricola spent his boyhood. The meagre ruins of the Roman town are uncomfortably hemmed in between city streets and the railway at the east end of the lower town.

GIARDINI BOTANICI HANBURY

By far the finest attraction in Ventimiglia, not to be missed, is the splendid green oasis of the Giardini Botanici Hanbury on the cape of La Mortola, west of the historic town centre and a stone's throw from the French border. This remarkable mosaic of botanic gardens (*open 9.30–6 in spring/autumn, until 7pm in summer, 5pm in winter; last entry 1hr before closing; www.giardinihanbury.com*) was founded in 1867 by Sir Thomas Hanbury, a merchant who made his fortune in the Orient, and his brother Daniel, a botanist. Here, in what is universally considered the most remarkable *jardin d'acclimatation* of the riviera, are exotic plants from all over the world (particularly from Asia and Africa) perfectly integrated with umbrella pines and cypresses, carob trees and palms, medicinal herbs and citrus fruits. Hanbury exposed a section of the Roman Via Aurelia at the foot of the gardens by the sea, and a plaque recalls famous travellers who passed along this route (including Dante, Machiavelli and Pius VII). The gardens are administered by the University of Genoa, whereas the lovely warm red Hanbury villa, used for meetings and exhibitions, is run by the Fine Arts Authority of Liguria. The garden shop sells seeds and plants, and if you are a researcher, or would like simply to volunteer your services as a gardener, you can arrange a stay in the lovely little *foresteria*.

GRIMALDI, DOLCEACQUA AND PIGNA

Having come this far from the highway (or the station) you may want to continue on to the **Balzi Rossi**, the red-rock cliffs overlooking the beach near the frontier village of Grimaldi (*map A, A2*). Here are several caves where relics of Palaeolithic inhabitants, dating as far back as 240,000 years ago, were discovered in 1892. Lovely new pathways enable you to visit the caves, and some of the finds are exhibited in the Museo Nazionale Preistorico (*open Tues–Sun 8.30–7.30*), founded here in 1898 by Sir Thomas Hanbury.

Driving inland from Ventimiglia, in the Val Nervia, takes you instead to a very different Liguria, a place of luxuriant forests, terraced olive groves and vineyards, and sometimes frighteningly steep mountainsides. Here lies the pretty village of **Dolceacqua** (*map A, A2*) beneath its splendid castle, first built in the 10th–11th century, transformed in the 15th and 16th centuries by the Doria, abandoned in the 18th century and recently restored as an exhibition and events centre. The award-winning 2007 design by Andrea Folli includes an open-air theatre in the Cortile d'Onore and a glass-enclosed auditorium on the castle walls. A single-arched 15th-century bridge spans the Nervia at the foot of the village. Fifteen minutes (11km) further on is **Pigna** (*map A, A1*), another little village, with a 15th-century polyptych by Giovanni Canavesio in the church of San Michele; built on an interesting plan, it stands in a picturesque position opposite the fortified village of **Castel Vittorio**. The area along the French border here is one of several comprising the **Parco Naturale Regionale delle Alpi Liguri** (*www.parks.it/parco.alpi.liguri*), and Pigna is a starting point for challenging but beautiful hikes along the Ligurian High Trail, the Alta Via dei Monti Liguri.

BORDIGHERA

This winter resort (*map A, A2*) became known in Britain after 1855, when *Doctor Antonio*, by the novelist and Risorgimento patriot Giovanni Ruffini, became a best-seller; the story was set in Bordighera and by the end of the 19th century a large English colony had been established here. Bordighera is also known through the paintings of Monet, who lived at the Pension Anglaise (now defunct) and worked *en plein air* in the surrounding countryside, producing some 50 canvases in the winter of 1884. 'Everything is marvellous, the countryside is more beautiful every day and I'm completely enchanted', he wrote to the Paris collector and dealer Paul Durand-Ruel. 'Beauty is everywhere and the weather is superb.'

Monet was the second Frenchman to give Bordighera a place in the history of art: the architect Charles Garnier (Paris Opéra, Montecarlo Casino, Nice Observatory) designed several buildings in the town in the 1870s: Villa Etelinda (originally Bischoffsheim), the Town Hall (originally a school), the Chiesa di Terrasanta, Villa Studio and his own home, Villa Garnier. On Via Romana, the villa in which Queen Margherita of Savoy (widow of Umberto I) died in 1926, faces the **Museo Bicknell** (*open Mon 8.30–1 & 1.30–5, Tues–Thur 9–1*), founded in 1888 by Bordighera's most eccentric English resident, the painter, botanist, mathematician and pastor Clarence Bicknell. The museum, home to the Istituto Internazionale di Studi Liguri, has good (if small) natural history and archaeological collections. It's a pity Monet left Bordighera before the immense wisteria that guards the entrance was planted. Bicknell also founded the International Library, at Via Romana 30.

The tiny historic centre, **Bordighera Alta**, is a fortified village surrounded by medieval walls reinforced in the 16th century. The village is still accessed through three gates and criss-crossed by a network of streets and squares arranged around the two main streets, the Via Lunga and Via Dritta. Most of the houses are connected by arches built after the earthquake that shook the city in 1887.

Bordighera has the northernmost colony of date palms (*Phoenix dactylifera*) in the world. The trees were first planted, according to one theory, by the Phoenicians.

SAN REMO

The largest summer and winter resort on the Italian Riviera, San Remo (*map A, A2*) has been visited since the mid-19th century for its superb climate. Its location is particularly amenable, facing due south for maximum sun and warmth, and the city's villas and gardens lie in an amphitheatre in a wide bay. The sea was once separated from the town by the old railway line, but in 2005–2010 this was ripped out to make a beautiful walkway and cycling path that now extends all the way from Ospedaletti, west of San Remo, to San Lorenzo al Mare, a suburb of Imperia. The 24km segment is the first of several that will eventually connect Ventimiglia to Genoa. Today the town is famous for its annual festivals, especially the International Song Contest.

In the late 19th and early 20th centuries notables from all over Europe came to winter in San Remo. English artist, illustrator, author and poet Edward Lear (1812–88) spent his last years here and built the Villa Emily (now Villa Verde) and Villa Tennyson, both named after Tennyson's wife; he died at the latter and was buried in San Remo. The empress of Russia, Maria Alexandrovna, consort of Alexander II, lived here, surrounded after 1874 by a large Russian colony, and toward the end of the seventies Tchaikovsky installed himself in the town, following the disintegration of his marriage to Antonina Miliukova. Alfred Nobel, the Swedish inventor and founder of the Nobel Prize (1833–96), also spent his last years here. The **Villa Nobel**, with a lovely garden, can be reached directly from the foot- and bike-path and holds a small museum (*open*

Tues–Sun 10–12.30; Fri–Sun and holidays also 3–6) devoted to Nobel himself ('If I come up with 300 ideas a year and only one is realisable, I'm happy') and his times.

From Villa Nobel the foot-and bike-path leads west, between the Public Gardens and the Porto Sole, now the yacht basin. A few metres west of the latter, on the beach, is the sleek Modern **Stabilimento Balneare Morgana**, built during the 1930s as part of a project to complete the esplanade developed between 1887 and 1888 by Giuseppe Poggi. The recently restored building, with its curved windows, helicoidal staircase and stout tower, was conceived by Rationalist architect Aldo Morando in 1936 and is still San Remo's most fashionable bathing establishment.

At the northeast end of Corso Matteotti, San Remo's elegant shopping street, is the 16th-century Palazzo Borea d'Olmo, home to the **Museo Civico Archeologico e Pinacoteca** (*Via Matteotti 143; open Tues–Sat 9–7*), displaying antiquities and paintings in its monumental interior. There are finds from prehistory to the Roman age here, and some 17th- and 18th-century frescoes (by Giovanni Battista Merano and Maurizio Carrega, respectively), but perhaps the most intriguing exhibit is the correspondence between Giuseppe Garibaldi and the young Englishwoman Caroline Giffard Phillipson, preserved in the section devoted to local history. 'Dear and gentle lady, I love you with all the affection of which I am capable', Garibaldi wrote to Mrs Phillipson on 14th October 1867; she in her turn asked for—and obtained—a lock of his hair.

Walk southwest along Corso Matteotti to reach San Remo's most celebrated building, the **Casinò Municipale** (*always open*), an Art Nouveau edifice by Eugène Ferret (1904–6) surrounded by gardens. Via Nino Bixio leads east from the Casinò to the Genoese fort of **Santa Tecla** (1755), an imposing triangular fortress that is slowly being transformed into a museum of local history and an events centre. The historic district of **La Pigna**, on a knoll northwest of the fort, has quaint narrow streets and tiny city blocks resembling the scales of a pine cone, hence the name. Here is the cathedral of **San Siro**, a 13th-century building enlarged in the 17th century. Across the cathedral square is the beautiful little **Oratorio dell'Immacolata Concezione**, a Baroque chapel of the 17th century and the only church in the area with an interior entirely faced in polychrome marble; it has recently reopened after a delicate restoration that took four years to complete (2006–10). There are ceiling frescoes by G.B. Merano (*God the Father with Angels and Prophets*, c. 1695) in the presbytery and G.B. Palmari (*Madonna Immacolata*, 1632) in the nave, and ten large canvases in marble frames representing the *Life of the Virgin* on the walls.

ENVIRONS OF SAN REMO

The environs of San Remo are at least as interesting as the city itself, and a good deal less hectic. On the western outskirts, at Via Padre Semeria 191, the **Monastero del Carmelo di Sant'Elia** (*open daily 8–6; T: 0184 660 470 to reserve a visit*) stands on high ground in a spot that was probably chosen for its isolation and silence. Designed by Gio Ponti in 1958 for the Discalced Carmelite nuns, it comprises a walled enclosure, a church and areas for meditation. Throughout the complex Ponti equates religious spirituality with simplicity of form, surface and colour, 'dematerialising' the architecture to create a serene, meditative environment. The interiors are uniformly white with fine blue glass detailing and a very few works of art, notably a painting of the *Madonna of Mercy* and an enamel panel with episodes from the life of the prophet Elijah, by Romano Ruiz. The form of the Cross appears throughout the convent—in the columns of the cloister, the framework of the church windows, etc.—and the long, white convent wall was intended to be covered with foliage. In the architect's words, 'this architecture needs time, rain and sunshine, and trees, grass and climbing plants need to grow for it to be what I had in mind'. The 'thick, penetrating greenery' Ponti imagined unfortunately never materialised, but the nuns have kept the original furniture, also designed by Ponti. The convent shop (*open 9–12 & 3–5.30*) sells the sisters' homemade fruit and vegetable preserves, all created with produce from the convent garden and citrus groves, and rightly famous.

Rising on a knoll just east of San Remo is the ruined village of **Bussana Vecchia**, destroyed by the earthquake of 1887. Long abandoned, it was taken over in the 1960s by a group of artists and craftspeople who rebuilt it from the rubble, placing stone upon stone. Later gentrified, it has lost its 60s' 'edge' and is now simply a pleasant place for an afternoon stroll.

TAGGIA AND TRIORA

Nearby **Taggia** (*map A, A2*) is an interesting old village in a pretty position. The 15th-century Gothic church of San Domenico contains works by Lodovico Brea; the convent houses a small museum (*open Tues–Sun 9–11.30 & 3–5*) displaying paintings, sculpture, manuscripts, miniatures and prints ranging in date from the 14th–18th centuries. In the old walled town is a palace attributed to Gian Lorenzo Bernini, and the parish church may also have been designed by him. A 16th-century **bridge** (on Romanesque foundations) of 16 arches crosses the Torrente Argentina. The tiny but tasty *olive taggiasche* are valued highly by gourmets in Italy and abroad. A word of caution: they are extremely moreish.

At the head of the pretty Valle Argentina, a 40-min drive from Taggia, is **Triora** (*map A, A1*), a medieval village with remains of its fortifications, a *Baptism of Christ* by Taddeo di Bartolo (1397) in the Collegiata and lively 15th-century frescoes in the little church of San Bernardino. A picturesque place with narrow little alleys and houses that seem to tumble down the hillside, it is sadly famous for the witchcraft trials of 1587–9, which led to the execution of six local women; the story is told in a little museum of witches and witchcraft (*open July–Sept daily 10.30–12 & 3–6.30; Oct–June daily 2.30–6 or 6.30, Sat, Sun & holidays also 10.30–12*) which also has an ethnographic collection focusing on peasant life. The town is a good starting point for hikes along the Alta Via dei Monti Liguri, the Ligurian High Trail (*www.altaviadeimontiliguri.it/portale*).

IMPERIA AND ONEGLIA

The rambling provincial capital of Imperia (*map A, B2*) was created in 1923 by the fusion of Porto Maurizio, Oneglia and adjoining villages. A few years back the plan to create an immense new marina offered a golden opportunity to sew the patchwork urban fabric together using a shared waterfront as the *trait d'union*. But little was done to tie the new infrastructure to its setting, and today the marina stands alone, in splendid isolation, between Porto Maurizio on the west and Oneglia on the east. It is a pity, because Imperia is a very pretty town with a great deal of potential.

Porto Maurizio has an old district of stepped streets, *caruggi* and *creuze*, on the slopes of the Parasio peninsula. Wandering around here is a real treat: although there are no masterpieces of art or architecture, there are several fine patrician palaces (Palazzo Lavagna, Palazzo Pagliari) and churches (San Pietro, Convento di Santa Chiara and, down by the water, Chiesa dei Cavalieri di Malta, of 1362). The **Collegiata di San Maurizio** (1781–1832), which dominates the skyline, is too big and too cold for its context (one wonders if a richer colour wouldn't help resolve the conflict), though the Neoclassical interior is admittedly impressive. The spacious square outside, the focal point of the 19th-century redesign of the historic town centre, is treated simply as an immense car park, in a manner more appropriate to the Italy of the 1950s. Across the piazza from the Collegiata, the **Museo Navale Internazionale del Ponente Ligure** (*open Wed and Sat, summer 9–11pm, winter 3.30–7.30*) is jam-packed with ship models, dioramas and other exhibits about sailing. Here too is the newly reinstalled **Museo del Presepe & Pinacoteca Civica** (*open Wed, Sat, Sun, summer 9pm–midnight, winter 4–7*), the centrepiece of which is a huge and wonderful Christmas crib with 113 carved wood figurines (81 people and 32 animals) ranging from 22 to 52cm in height and, in most cases, dressed in rich colourful costumes. The **Stabilimento Balneare Spiaggia d'Oro**, on Porto Maurizio's 'golden beach', was designed by Alfredo Campanini in 1913, in a Viennese Secessionist style with ceramic and glazed majolica inserts on the façades. The original ballroom, on the upper level, is now used for private parties and concerts.

ONEGLIA

Oneglia (*map A, B2*) lies at the mouth of the Impero torrent, from which the town of Imperia takes its name. It is an important centre of the olive-oil trade, and has a large pasta factory on the seafront. The **Museo dell'Olivo** (*Via Garessio 13, open Mon–Sat 9–12.30 & 3–6.30, www.museodellolivo.com*) offers displays regarding olive oil, its production and uses. The museum was created in 1992 by the Carli family, founders of a well-known oil firm, and is housed in their Art Nouveau corporate headquarters in the midst of the Carli presses and warehouses. Highlights of this unusual private collection are Babylonian clay tablets with cuneiform contracts and accounts regarding the sale of oil (2nd millennium BC), various Egyptian, Greek and Roman vessels for oil and cosmetics, historic tools and equipment for pressing oil, and a rebuilt Roman ship showing how amphorae were stowed for long-haul transport.

Villa Grock, in the hills at the intersection of Via Fanny Roncati Carli e Via Grock (*10mins on foot or by car from the Museo dell'Olivo*), was the home of Grock (Adrien Wettach), the great Swiss clown, who died in 1959 in the eclectic mansion. The villa and its exuberant garden now host an interactive museum dedicated to circuses and, particularly, to clowns, whose child-friendly displays are perfectly in tune with the overall playfulness of the premises (*open Sat and Sun, summer 5–8, winter 3–6; www.museodelclown.it*).

Imperia's Chamber of Commerce is housed in the former **Oleificio Sasso**, the corporate headquarters of another important oil firm, at Via De Sonnaz 21. The building was designed in 1923 by Alfonso Sholl in the retro-Modern Novecento style and restored by Paola Muratorio in 2012.

Oneglia's little **harbour** still has an air of days gone by, with fishing boats and restaurants serving the day's catch along the quay.

LINGUELIETTA

In the hills due west of Imperia is Linguelietta (*map A, A2*), once an austere stone farming village, now a cluster of second homes inhabited almost exclusively in summer. The views make the drive up worthwhile, though the overall atmosphere of the village's lanes and alleys is spoiled by an excessive cultivation of the picturesque. At the landward end of the village, authenticity returns with a vengeance in the fortified church of **San Pietro**. There are only five churches of this kind in Italy, and this one is among the finest. Built in the 12th or 13th century (one supposes, judging from the Romanesque apse and the square-cut masonry of the lower walls, a technique that was later abandoned because too costly), it was fortified in the 16th century, its dominant position over the village and the surrounding countryside making it a perfect refuge from the Barbary pirates who terrorised the Riviera di Ponente around 1550. Now deconsecrated, it was beautifully restored as a visual and performing arts space in 2012, to designs by Luca Dolmetta.

CERVO

Cervo (*map A, B2*) is quite simply one of the most beautiful villages in Italy. Its picturesque streets, colourful houses and stunning sea views have earned it the nickname *Paradiso dei pittori*, 'painters' paradise'. Its summer chamber-music festival, held in the square in front of the Baroque church of St John the Baptist overlooking the sea and coast, is internationally famous.

Clustered on a headland directly above the sea, the village follows a typically medieval plan, with parallel streets running north to south connected by lanes and narrow stairways. Its weathered beauty, a mix of pastel-coloured walls adorned with brilliant flowers and verdant creepers, and cobbled streets too narrow for cars, make it one of the most charming places on the coast. The upper, inland end of the village is the oldest; many of the two- or three-floor houses here have arches embedded in the ground-floor walls, suggesting that the lanes may have been covered by porticoes. The lower part of the village, which dates from the 17th century, is speckled with stately Baroque mansions. Noticeably, the historic village centre has no modern buildings or asphalted streets, stone being the paving material.

Cervo's origins date back to Roman times, when it was a *mansio*, or official stopping place, along the Via Julia Augusta. It was a fief of the marquis of Clavesana in the 11th century, but was soon brought under the jurisdiction of the Republic of Genoa, which gave it the ramparts and bastions you see today. Until quite recently the economy was based on fishing and farming. Since the 1960s, though, these activities have been largely supplanted by tourism, with the consequent flourishing of restaurants, cafés and craft shops. Fortunately Cervo's 1,200 residents have held on stubbornly to their old ways—which means the restaurants still serve the morning catch, garnished with vine-ripened tomatoes and other local produce and dressed with olive oil cold-pressed within a stone's throw of the village. Menus, as you might expect, are strictly Mediterranean.

EXPLORING CERVO

The usual entrance to the town is from its highest point by one of two gates in the old walls. In the little piazza here stands the **Clavesana castle**, which dates as least as far back as 12th century. Originally built to defend the population against Saracen pirates, the rectangular stone fortress subsequently became a church dedicated to St Catherine of Alexandria and then a hospital. It is still an important example of medieval Ligurian military architecture, notwithstanding these transformations and other, smaller changes made over the years. Today it hosts the Visitors' Information Office and the **Museo Etnografico del Ponente Ligure** (*open Mon–Sat summer 9–12 & 3.30–7, winter 9–12 & 3–4.30*), which features objects from 19th-century home- and work-life displayed in reconstructed interiors peopled by amusing *papier-mâché* mannequins.

From the castle, the three main streets, Via Salineri and the parallel Via Cavour and Via Volta, all descend to the parish church of **San Giovanni Battista**. Villagers call it the *Chiesa dei Corallini*, because it was financed with the proceeds from the sale of coral gathered by local fishermen off the coasts of Corsica and Sardinia. The most important Baroque building of western Liguria, the church stands theatrically on a high parvis overlooking the sea, its concave pink-and-blue façade adorned with pilaster strips, niches and arabesques. The main body of the building was designed by a local architect, Giovanni Battista Marvaldi, in the late 17th century; the soaring campanile was added by another local, painter Francesco Carrega, a century later. The single-aisled interior, with rounded corners and five chapels on each side, has a 14th-century white marble pulpit, a polychrome wood sculpture of *The Family of St John* (of uncertain attribution) on the south side, a ceiling fresco by Francesco Carrega in the presbytery, and a Crucifix by local artist Anton Maria Maragliano on the fourth north altar.

A little below San Giovanni is the **Oratory of Santa Caterina**, established as a private chapel in the 13th century, made into a parish church in the 16th century, and now an exhibition space and concert hall. It has a fine main portal combining Romanesque and Gothic elements. Here too the interior is a simple, rectangular hall. It is adorned with anonymous 16th-century frescoes, including a large *St George and the Dragon* on the west wall, over the main doorway.

Further downhill are the 17th-century Palazzo Morchio, now the Town Hall, and the early 18th-century **Palazzo Viale**. The latter was the residence of one of Cervo's most prominent families, which derived its wealth from farming and shipping. Built along the then-new Napoleonic highway from Paris to Rome, it has stuccoed and painted decorations on the outside and a white marble portal. The interior has two 'master' floors—one more than usual—having been designed to accommodate four brothers and their families. Today the second master floor, painted by Francesco Carrega with scenes of myth and allegory, is used for cultural events.

The most important of these events, and one that shouldn't be missed, is Cervo's **International Chamber Music Festival**. Established by the Hungarian violinist Sándor Végh in 1964, it is held annually in July and August and is one of the leading chamber music events in Europe. In the past it has drawn performers of the calibre of violinists Uto Ughi, Salvatore Accardo and Yehudi Menuhin, and pianists Maurizio Pollini, Arturo Benedetti Michelangeli and Sviatoslav Richter, to name just a few. Associated with the festival is an International Summer Academy for young musicians.

THE RIVIERA DELLE PALME

Although there are palms here, the distinguishing feature of this stretch of coast is industry—doubtless less likely to attract visitors than tall exotic trees. To be exact one should speak not of industry but of craft, practised on a large scale and at an extremely high level of competence. Shipbuilding—and ship breaking—made the fortune of Savona, and ceramics that of Albissola. The potters of Albissola and its neighbouring towns are world renowned. West of Savona, agriculture is the traditional occupation, as on the Riviera dei Fiori, and the towns and countryside still retain a strong feudal imprint.

ALASSIO

One of the most popular Ligurian coastal resorts, Alassio (*map A, B2*) has an exceptionally mild winter climate and an excellent sandy beach. It is at the head of a wide, beautiful bay, facing nearly east. It was well known to the English by the end of the 19th century (they built the church of St John's, now used for exhibitions and concerts) and is famed for the luxuriance of its gardens. While wintering here in 1904, Sir Edward Elgar composed his overture *In the South (Alassio)*. Carlo Levi, the writer and painter, spent much time in Alassio, and 22 of his bright, Expressionistic paintings are exhibited in the **Pinacoteca** at Palazzo Morteo (*Via Gramsci 58, open June–Sept Thur 5.30–7.30, Fri 9–11pm, Sat, Sun and holidays 5–7.30 and 9–11pm; Sept–May Fri, Sat, Sun and holidays 3–6*). These include a fine collection of Riviera landscapes and a splendid 1961 portrait of Italo Calvino. A showcase displays Levi's manuscripts, notes and letters, donated to the city by Silvia and Antonio Ricci and first presented to the public in 2014.

Alassio is known in popular culture for its *muretto*, originally an anonymous retaining wall along the Giardini Pubblici, later adorned, at the initiative of Mario Berrino, proprietor of the historic **Caffè Roma** across the street, with ceramic tiles signed by the café's celebrity clients. It seems the first to sign was a certain Ernest Hemingway. Now there are more than 1,000 tiles. If you look closely you can find the signatures of actress Anita Ekberg, playwright Jean Cocteau, Nobel Prize actor and playwright Dario Fo, explorer Thor Heyerdahl, poets Jacques Prévert and Salvatore Quasimodo, and many more.

Alassio's waterfront terrace, **Piazza Airaldi Durante**, with its wooden pavement and soft, colourful night lighting, was designed by Luca Dolmetta in 2009. Adjoining the church of Sant'Anna, it offers a much-needed connection between the main shopping street, Via Vittorio Veneto, and the beach.

Offshore is the **Isola Gallinara**, or Gallinaria (*boat trips from the marina or from Loano, map A, B2*). Little remains of the once powerful Benedictine monastery founded here in the 8th century, which at one time owned most of the Riviera di Ponente. St Martin of Tours took refuge from his Arian persecutors here in 356–60. The island is now privately owned; it has been a nature reserve since 1989, with grottoes, lovely vegetation and interesting birdlife.

ALBENGA

Albenga (*map A, B2*) was the Roman port *Albium Ingaunum*, but is now over a kilometre from the sea, as the course of its river, the Centa, was altered in the 13th century. It still has most of its medieval walls (on foundations of the 1st century BC) and three 17th-century gates; also about a dozen 12th–14th-century brick tower-houses, mostly well restored. The town has expanded towards the sea since the 19th century and now has a very popular palm-shaded beachfront.

The cathedral of **San Michele Arcangelo**, on late 4th- or early 5th-century foundations, with an elegant campanile of 1391, was restored to its medieval forms in 1967. The interior, with its basilican plan and pointed arches borne by robust columns, dates from the late 12th or early 13th century, but was altered in the 16th century when the floor was raised 1m, the columns were reinforced, the ogival arches were redesigned and the vaults and domes were added to the ceilings. The 20th-century restoration removed the changes to the floor and arches (as well as the Baroque decorations of the sanctuary). The ceiling frescoes were added in the 19th century by Maurizio and Tommaso Carrega, Santo Bertelli and Raffaele Resio. There are 15th-century frescoes of saints in the sanctuary, a 15th-century *Pentecost* in the south apse, and a 16th-century paliotto with *Sts Veranus of Vence, Michael and John the Baptist* over the high altar; all are by unknown artists. The 5th-century **baptistery**, ten-sided without and octagonal within, preserves a fine Byzantine mosaic of the 5th or 6th century in its principal apse and 8th-century transennae.

The charming **Piazzetta dei Leoni** has a black and white pavement of inlaid cobblestones and three Renaissance lions brought from Rome in 1608. The former bishop's palace has external frescoes (15th century); the little diocesan museum inside contains finds from the cathedral and paintings by Guido Reni and Domenico Piola. The Palazzo Vecchio del Comune (1387 and 1421), incorporating a tall tower of c. 1300, houses the **Civico Museo Ingauno** (*open Tues–Sun summer 9.30–12 & 3.30–7.30, winter 10–12.30 & 2.30–6*) with well-displayed prehistoric, Roman and medieval remains. The epigraphic collection occupies the imposing Sala dei Consoli, the ground-floor hall of the Torre del Comune. Via Bernardo Ricci (the Roman *decumanus*) crosses Via Medaglie d'Oro (the *cardo maximus*) at the 13th-century Loggia dei Quattro Canti.

In Piazza San Michele, in the elegant Palazzo Oddo, is the **Museo Navale**

Romano (*open Tues–Sun, summer 9.30–12.30 & 3.30–7.30; winter 10–12.30 & 2.30–6*), containing more than 100 wine amphorae and marine fittings salvaged since 1950 from a Roman vessel sunk offshore in 100–90 BC. This is the largest Roman transport ship yet found in the Mediterranean; it was carrying more than 10,000 amphorae of wine (700 of which were recovered) from Campania to southern France and Spain. Attached to the museum is an important centre for underwater archaeology. In a fine 18th-century hall there is a collection of Albissola pharmacy jars. You can see scanty remains of the Roman city along the River Centa.

ZUCCARELLO AND COLETTA DI CASTELBIANCO

You shouldn't leave Albenga without taking a morning or afternoon to explore its lush, green hinterland. Nestled on the left bank of the Torrente Neva half an hour from beach is **Zuccarello** (*map A, B2*), an absolutely delightful place with one main street and a number of picturesque *caruggi*. Low porticoes flank the main street, with its pastel-coloured houses, and a little Romanesque bridge crosses rushing waters of the Neva. There are also two small churches: the richly decorated San Bartolomeo, and Santa Maria Nascente with a tall Romanesque campanile. Peace and quiet rule here, and if you have toddlers in tow you can cut them loose without a worry. The signature dish of Zuccarello is *torta pasqualina* (traditionally made for Easter but now available throughout the spring), a flaky pastry stuffed with wild herbs, milk curd, parmesan and eggs.

A paved footpath (*marked*) climbs in 15mins to the ruined 13th-century castle on the hill above the town, from which a ridge-top trail (3km; the trail is named after Ilaria del Carretto, the wife of Pietro Guinigi, lord of Lucca, who was born in Zucarello in 1379 and whose statue stands by the seaward gate of the village) leads through chestnut woods in c. 1hr to **Castelvecchio di Rocca Barbena**. Nestled on its hilltop at the foot of an 11th-century fortress and enjoying breathtaking views, this is the oldest and most impressive of the walled villages of the Val di Neva; the village streets are narrow and stony, the houses connected by arches, an early anti-seismic measure. The external bread ovens are a characteristic feature, as are the white frames around the doors and windows, in the Provençal-Alpine tradition. There is also a road up to Castelvecchio, but it's not recommended unless you wish to tempt your fate.

At Martinetto a road diverges west to **Coletta di Castelbianco** (*map A, B2*), another stony village with white-framed doors and windows and flat, terraced rooftops. It is the prettiest of four villages in a little amphitheatre of mountains, the steep walls of which are popular with rock-climbers. It has a certain reputation amongst gourmets for its two indigenous varieties of cherry: *Cantun Giancau* and *Cantun Negrau*. The black truffles found in the woods between Zuccarello, Castelvecchio and Castelbianco are also justly famous.

FINALE LIGURE

This town (*map A, C2*) is known for its lovely palm-shaded seaside promenade, but the real draws are in the environs. The old walled village of **Finalborgo**, 2km inland from Finale Marina, is one of the best preserved on the coast. It has a church with a fine octagonal campanile (13th century) and a 16th-century tomb of the Del Carretto family, whose ruined castle is nearby. In the cloister of Santa Caterina is the **Museo Archeologico del Finale** (*open Tues–Sun, summer 10–12 & 4–7; winter 9–12 & 2.30–5, www.museoarcheologicodelfinale.it*), with material from the Palaeolithic to the Middle Ages, including finds from the many local limestone caves in which prehistoric remains have been discovered. On the old Roman road further inland are about a dozen Roman bridges (1st century AD), five of them intact.

A twisting, turning road climbs from the Via Aurelia west of Finale to **Borgio Verezzi**, and although the drive up can be harrowing (a bit of manoeuvring is almost almost necessary, to let oncoming vehicles by), what you find when you get there makes it all worthwhile. This medieval village perched on its hillside overlooking the sea is actually a cluster of four smaller hamlets: Poggio, Piazza, Roccaro and Crosa. You must leave your car at the entrance to the village and proceed on foot along the *caruggi* and *creuze*. The houses, some with water-catching flat roofs of Saracenic inspiration, seem to spring directly from the underlying rock, which can be seen peeping through the greenery here and there. The whole effect is almost overwhelming in spring and early summer when the flowers, wild and cultivated, are in bloom. The sea views are superb in all seasons, particularly at sunset. The Festival Teatrale di Borgio Verezzi, with open-air performances in the little Piazza Sant'Agostino, takes place in July. Another festival, in mid-August, focuses on *lumache alla verezzina*, Borgio Verezzi's locally famous stewed-snail dish.

NOLI AND BERGEGGI

An important port in the Middle Ages, this pretty little seaside town (*map A, C2*) preserves its walls and three tall towers of brick, as well as some old houses, a beautifully tended waterfront garden and an 11th-century church. With the exception of the church, all the sights in Noli are easily seen from the outside, so the main thing to do is just stroll around and drink up the atmosphere—which is very pleasant indeed.

One interpretation of the name traces the town's foundation back to Byzantine times, deriving Noli from the Greek *neapolis*, 'new town'. The **town walls** and their gates date from the 12th–13th century, as do the more important buildings: the Palazzo Comunale and the tall Torre del Comune, at the centre of the old town, and the **ruined castle** of the Marchesi Del Carretto on its hilltop to the north (although the castle was altered by the Genoese in the 16th century). Opposite the Palazzo Comunale is the double-arched **Loggia della Repubblica**—a reminder that Noli was once an independent maritime republic. The church of San Pietro is a Romanesque foundation made over in the Baroque period; it has been Noli's cathedral since 1572, taking the role over from **San Paragorio**, at the extreme south end of the town. This early Romanesque construction, flanked by medieval tombs, may be the oldest extant monument on this stretch of the riviera. The austere interior has a beautiful apse, raised presbytery and crypt; the *Volto Santo*, a wooden Crucifix in a 12th-century Byzantine style, is much venerated locally. On a knoll at the north end of the old town stands the Palazzo Vescovile, begun in the 15th century but given its present form in the 18th; it is now a hotel. The adjoining church of Nostra Signora delle Grazie was built in the 17th century but altered in 1769.

BERGEGGI

Northeast of Noli, beyond the busy resort of Spotorno (undoubtedly a quieter place when D.H. Lawrence visited in 1926) lies Bergeggi (*map A, C2*), a pleasant village on a headland 100m above its beach, with the little Isola di Bergeggi (or di Sant'Eugeneo) offshore. The islet and the waters around it are now a nature reserve, where walking, swimming and kayaking are welcome, but motor vehicles and motor boats are not. The *macchia mediterranea* on the island is particularly fragrant on warm, sunny days.

SAVONA

Savona (*map A, C2*) is a tough working town in the midst of a region increasingly devoted to leisure. The first thing one wants to do here, is leave: the old town is too dark, the 19th-century city is too solemn, and the 20th-century industrial and working-class residential neighbourhoods remind one of the places one came here to forget. But then something happens. Step out of your car or off the train (the 20th-century engineer Pier Luigi Nervi, designer of the Papal Audience Hall in the Vatican City and the Pirelli Building in Milan, designed the station) and the town becomes interesting. There is a buzz in the air, an energy. It's the people that make Savona. Proud, industrious and generous, they carry forward an intellectual and entrepreneurial tradition that makes the other provincial capital of this riviera, Imperia, look like a sleepy country village.

Savona was first settled about 7,000 years ago and has felt a rivalry with Genoa ever since. It sided with Carthage in the Second Punic War (Genoa allied with Rome), achieving a memorable victory over its rival, but Rome's ultimate defeat of Carthage forced the city into the shadow of nearby *Vada Sabatia* (the modern Vado Ligure), a Roman town that also had the good fortune to stand at the junction between the road to Genoa and that over the Alps. Today Vado is still Savona's main cargo port, and the place where most heavy industry is concentrated.

In the early Middle Ages Savona became a base of the Byzantine fleet and the little knoll of Priamàr, the site of the original settlement, was made the seat of a bishop and given a proper fortress. This was Savona's first real moment of splendour; it developed its civic institutions and commercial base, and gradually built a merchant fleet, becoming a regional trade hub thanks to the good offices of the Byzantines.

The Byzantine city was levelled in 643, however, by the Lombard Rothair, in the first of the waves of destruction that characterised the later centuries of the first millennium. In the 11th century Savona again rose up to become a busy port and an important centre of trade with Northern Europe, once more in competition with Genoa. In 1191 it became a free commune and the urban fabric began to spread beyond the Priamàr hill to the lowlands by the old harbour, the centre of economic life. From the 13th to the 15th century this area witnessed the building of the first bourgeois tower houses (such as the **Torri del Brandale**, overlooking the pleasant little square that is now Savona's most popular meeting-point), followed by the great palaces, the most sumptuous of which is the unfinished **Palazzo Della Rovere**, the splendid Renaissance building designed by Giuliano da Sangallo for Giuliano Della Rovere, opposite the cathedral, a stone's throw from Piazza del Brandale.

This was undoubtedly Savona's finest hour, a period in which its maritime republic was able to hold its own, commercially and militarily, against Genoa and her allies.

SAVONA AND ITS POPES

The economic boom of the late 15th century was aided by a number of factors, not least of which the election to the papacy of two eminent citizens, Francesco Della Rovere (Sixtus IV, pope from 1471 to 1484), and his nephew Giuliano Della Rovere (Julius II, 1503–13). Both were among the most active art patrons of the Renaissance (Sixtus is often credited with being the first to bring the new art to Rome). In addition to commissioning the Vatican chapel that bears his name (later frescoed by Michelangelo at the command of his nephew), Sixtus built a little oratory here to honour the memory of his parents. Savona's **Capella Sistina** stands across the square from the family palace, next to the much later (and uninteresting) cathedral; it was given its harmonious Baroque interior in 1764 and contains a fine marble tomb, by Michele and Giovanni de Aria, with figures of the two Della Rovere popes. At Julius' initiative, in 1507 a historic meeting took place here between Ferdinand II, King of Aragon, and Louis XII of France, to forge an alliance, the League of Cambrai, that might curb the growing power of the Republic of Venice.

The decline of Savona began in the second quarter of the 16th century: defeat at the hands of Genoa in 1528 brought the closure of the harbour, the razing of the Priamàr quarter and the partial destruction of the rest of the city. On the Priamàr hill the Genoese built the fortress one sees today—whose cannon, according to the story told locally, were pointed towards the city, not the sea. The population dwindled to a third of its former number and the town settled into a slumber destined to last nearly three centuries.

PINACOTECA CIVICA

Notwithstanding the downturn, or perhaps because of it, some families continued to prosper, and wandering the streets of the old city centre you can still see the odd Baroque or Rococo *palazzo*. One of these, the 17th-century Palazzo Gavotti, hosts the Pinacoteca Civica (*Piazza Chabrol; open Mon–Wed 10–1.30, Thur–Sat 10–1.30 & 3.30–6.30, Sun 10–1.30*), containing paintings, sculpture and ceramics from the Middle Ages to the present day; here are old-master paintings by Donato de Bardi (*Crucifixion with the Virgin, Mary Magdalene* and *St John the Baptist*), Vincenzo Foppa (*Pala Fornari*), Giovanni Battista Carlone, Giovanni Mazone, Orazio de Ferrari and Domenico Piola, among others, and Modern and contemporary works (on loan from the Milena Milani & Carlo Cardazzo Foundation) by Hans Arp, Alexander Calder, Giorgio de Chirico, Lucio Fontana, René Magritte, Joan Miró, Pablo Picasso, Man Ray, Cy Twombly and many others. There is also a fine, small collection of icons. Work is underway to create a dedicated space for the city's ceramics collection, together with several private collections of ceramics, including the extensive holdings of the local community foundation, in the adjacent Palazzo del Monte di Pietà; the two museums will be internally connected.

EIGHTEENTH–TWENTIETH-CENTURY SAVONA

In 1794 Savona became a hub of French operations against the Austro-Sardinian forces in Liguria and in 1796 Napoleon set up his headquarters in the bishop's palace here. With the annexation of Liguria to the French Empire in 1805 Savona became the capital of an administrative department; when the Treaty of Vienna assigned Liguria to the Kingdom of Piedmont, it managed to maintain its status as a centre of local government. Under the Savoy, and with the impetus of the Industrial Revolution, the city enjoyed an economic renaissance; the **new town** was built, its pattern of straight, regular streets based on that of Turin, of which Savona became the principal port. Locked up in the fortress of Priamàr in 1831 for his subversive political ideas, Giuseppe Mazzini here formulated the idea of *Giovane Italia* (Young Italy), which he founded in Marseilles later that year; the movement's goal was to provoke a popular insurrection in the Italian states and the territories occupied by the Austrian Empire to create a unified Republic of Italy. This was just the first of several important political movements to grow up in Savona in the 19th century; Italy's socialist-inspired *Società di Mutuo Soccorso* (Mutual Aid Society) was established here in 1890 and the *Camera del Lavoro* (Chamber of Labour) in 1902.

A long tradition of pride in democracy and a strong workers' movement made Savona a hothouse of anti-Fascist activity in the second quarter of the 20th century. The city is known to Italians for the **1927 Savona Trial** in which patriots Ferruccio Parri, Carlo Rosselli and Alessandro Pertini (President of the Republic 1978–85), accused of helping socialist leader Filippo Turati escape to France the previous year, formally attacked the Fascist government as illegitimate—an attack upheld by the court, which recognised the 'extraordinary circumstances' (i.e. the atmosphere of political persecution) in which their crime (facilitating the escape of a wanted man) had been committed. As one might expect, the citizens of Savona were extremely active in the World War II Resistance movement; their action earned the entire city the Gold Medal for Military Valour.

PRIAMÀR AND ITS MUSEUMS

Today Savona's city limits extend into the hills and up and down to coast as far as Vado and Albissola, but for visitors the focus of interest is still the Priamàr hill and its Genoese fortress. The **Fortezza del Priamàr**, surrounded by verdant public gardens and beautifully restored in 2012–13, is home to two museums, both in the north-facing Palazzo della Loggia. The entrance to the fortress is approached by a long pedestrian bridge over the lawns, from Corso Mazzini.

The **Civico Museo Archeologico e della Città**, on the ground floor and first floor (*open June–Sept daily except Tues 10.30–3; Sept–Jun Wed–Fri 9.30–12.30 & 2.30–4.30, Sat–Mon 10.30–3*), combines the castle excavations and the material found in an intriguing chronological itinerary that includes rooms belonging both the Genoese fortress and to its medieval predecessor. The late-antique and early-medieval necropolis has been reconstructed and the material in the showcases dates as far back as the Bronze Age. The ceramic collections range from early-medieval Islamic items to Modern creations.

The **Museo Sandro Pertini & Renata Cuneo**, on the second floor (*open Sun and Mon 10.30–3*), displays the collections donated to the city by the former President of the Republic and by a well-known local artist. They are arranged in adjacent, but separate spaces in a long, vaulted hall, the works in the Pertini collection organised by artist and subject, and Cuneo's sculptures chronologically. The Pertini collection focuses on Italian and European Modernism, with significant works by Giorgio de Chirico, Filippo de Pisis, Renato Guttuso, Joan Miró, Giorgio Morandi, Gio Pomodoro, Aligi Sassu, Mario Sironi and Emilio Vedova, among others. Cuneo's sculptures, in bronze and raw and glazed terracotta—the latter made at the San Giorgio and Mazzotti manufactories in Albissola—are little known outside Liguria.

THE OLD HARBOUR AREA

An enormous effort is currently underway to make the area at the foot of the fortress—from the public gardens to the old harbour—the hub of the contemporary city, a place, like Marseilles' Vieux Port, where residents and visitors alike can soak up the sun and pass the time, admiring the views, hopping from museum to museum, shopping, or just sipping cappuccino in the open-air cafés. But whereas Marseilles' new waterfront is a carefully coordinated revitalisation of the city's innermost core conducted with the entire populace in mind, Savona's is a hotchpotch of loosely linked interventions that is much less successful.

The master plan for the **old harbour** hinges on the concept of making it a departure point for cruise ships—as always, in competition with Genoa. The plan was entrusted to the Spanish architect Ricardo Bofill, a specialist in transportation infrastructures, and took ten years (1993–2003) to develop. The underlying concept is unfortunately flawed, as modern cruise ships are far too large for spaces as tight as Savona's historic harbour, conceived and built for a very different kind of vessel. To claim the opposite is to gloss far too lightly over issues of safety, as a 2011 incident in Genoa harbour, in which a 40,000-tonne cargo ship toppled a control tower and killed those working in it, attests. The harbour plan at Savona has allowed the construction of a new passenger terminal, an immense crescent-shaped hotel and retail complex, and a cluster of tall condominium towers. With the exception of the terminal (a beautiful and functional building with a distinctive 'seagull wing' roofline, designed by Marco Censasorte) these new buildings are completely out of scale with the historic urban fabric and constitute a visual and physical barrier between the city and the sea. The project's supporters argue that the buildings are in scale with the ships—which may be true, but then the ships too are out of scale with the city, just as they are with its harbour. Fortunately, the quieter, less ambitious elements of the old harbour renovation are very successful. The redevelopment of Piazza del Brandale and the old harbour quays (2008), entrusted to the young Savona architect Silvia Dagna, has been a triumph. Piazza del Brandale, once an anonymous place of passage, is now a lovely urban terrace with a smooth stepped pavement, wooden seating and shady Peruvian pepper trees: a much-loved space for meetings, markets or 'social networking'. The new quayside has been partly resurfaced in warm wood and given a little deck that projects from the shoreline, as well as a pedestrian bridge over the yacht basin, offering new views of the harbour and the town; it begins at the foot of the 14th-century **Torre Pancaldo**, named after Leon Pancaldo of Savona, Magellan's 'Genoese' pilot. There is stone seating by the wall and the whole area is nicely lit at night. The bronze *Seaman* is by Renata Cuneo.

ALBISSOLA MARINA AND ALBISOLA SUPERIORE

Albissola Marina (*map A, D2*) lies on the coast right next to Savona, separated by the Sansobbia torrent from Albisola Superiore, originally set in the hills 1km inland but now also extending to the beach. The discrepancy in spelling is a mystery that geographers have yet to unravel. Both place names derive from *Alba Docilia*, the Roman settlement whose scant ruins can be seen near the railway station.

Ceramics is the traditional industry here, thanks to the abundant clay in the hills. In the early 20th century it became much more than a livelihood for the area's craftsmen, as word spread among avant-garde artists of the extraordinary ability of local potters and decorators to transform audacious designs into real, live objects.

That ceramics were—and are—an important craft here is evident as soon as you set foot in the town. All along the waterfront runs the **Lungomare degli Artisti** (1962–3), a kilometre-long mosaic by local, Italian and international artists. It was the brainchild of Italian painter Aligi Sassu, who happened to be on the town council when Albissola Marina decided to build a new seaside promenade. The mosaic, executed with the help of Adolfo Testa, the founder of the Artists' Circle, and ceramicist Tullio Mazzotti, whose contribution to 20th-century European art is described below, is made up of roughly five million tesserae arranged in 20 large (5m by 10m) panels separated by 'neutral' blue-and-white striped panels. Unfortunately the surface is extremely delicate: the triangular tesserae in the panels designed by the artists (the best known of whom are probably the Italians Giuseppe Capogrossi, Lucio Fontana and Aligi Sassu, and the Cuban Wilfredo Lam) and the rectangular ones in the others, both have a tendency to crack or pop out, making constant restoration a necessity. The problem has been obviated in the 2005 extension along the beach at Albisola Superiore, where the ceramic tiles have been transferred to the seating, which forms a continuous, wave-like bench. Both promenades lead past other Modern artworks, such as Lucio Fontana's spherical *Natura* sculptures, Leoncillo's *Monumento ai caduti di tutte le guerre* and Corrado Levi's *Omaggio al Mondo–Socle d'Albisola*, an upside-down pedestal on which the world 'stands'.

On the right (Albissola Marina) bank of the Sansobbia stands the **Fabbrica Casa Museo Giuseppe Mazzotti** (*Viale Matteotti 25/29; open Mon–Fri 8.30–12.30 & 2.30–7.30; Sat, Sun and holidays 9.30–12.30 & 3.30–7.30; www.gmazzotti1903.it*), the museum of one of Albissola's two world-renowned producers of avant-garde pottery and ceramic sculpture (the other is the Manifattura San Giorgio). It was established in 1903 by Giuseppe Mazzotti, but the first contacts with artists were established by his sons, Tullio and Torido. Tullio was a fine-arts ceramicist in his own right, a member of the Futurist movement and a close friend of Futurist theorist Filippo Tommaso Marinetti. It is he who is credited with introducing ceramics to the Futurist movement and, substantially, with putting Albissola on the map as a centre of fine-arts ceramic production. Marinetti gave him the pseudonym 'Tullio d'Albissola', with which he signed his unusually shaped and coloured pottery and sculpture, one of the highlights of the collection here. Torido Mazzotti looked after the business side of the enterprise and worked with visiting artists to develop the techniques they needed to translate their ideas into physical objects. Among those he helped were Futurists Enrico Prampolini and Fortunato Depero, Abstract Expressionists Asger Jorn and Karel Appel, and proto-Conceptualists Piero Manzoni and Lucio Fontana (who in a rare figurative moment created the extraordinary *Alligator* in the museum garden).

The live-in studio designed for Tullio in 1930 by the Bulgarian painter, designer and architect Nicolay Diulgheroff is a rare example of Futurist residential architecture and has survived without substantial alterations. The design is a medley of 'simplicity, logic, proportion and economy' (Diulgheroff) whose boldly geometric shapes are coded by function with colours chosen by the architect and produced by his patron. Details such as the bevelled corners, the staircase and the iron railings recall the Futurist theatre sets of Fortunato Depero

Surrounded by lovely gardens in the hills overlooking Albissola Marina is the **Museo del Centro Studi Asger Jorn**. This new house museum (*Via Garbiele D'Annunzio 6, open Fri and Sat 4.30–6.30, Sun 10–12 & 4.30–6.30*) was the home and studio of the Danish Abstract Expressionist Asger Jorn, a member of the COBRA (Copenhagen-Brussels-Amsterdam) group. Jorn came to Albissola in 1954, helped organise the International Ceramics Meetings that attracted leading artists from around the world, and at the Manifattura San Giorgio produced some of his best-known works, notably the panel for the Åarhus Lyceum (1958–9), the largest Modern ceramic work (90 m2, 1,250 pieces). Around 150 of his works are shown in the house and garden; the garden paths are paved with bits and pieces that didn't make it through the kiln.

Perhaps the most stimulating contemporary architectural work in the Albisole, and certainly one that repays a visit, is the **seaside promenade** between Albisola Superiore and neighbouring Celle Ligure. The old rail bed has been converted into a stunning promenade with sea views. The rehabilitation of the abandoned railway was carried out in tandem by two Savona architectural firms, 3S Studio and Voarino Cairo Voarino. It includes a walkway, a cantilevered observation deck and an exhibition space in a former tunnel. The project won the PAI Architectural Award for infrastructure in 2012.

PRACTICAL TIPS

WHERE TO STAY ON THE RIVIERA DI PONENTE

ALASSIO (*map A, B2*)
€€€ **Villa della Pergola.** He is a television producer with a number of succesful shows to his credit, she is an art historian with years of experience in the Italian National Fine Arts Authority: together they have invested their wits, energy and financial resources in the examplary renovation of a magnificent property in the hills of Alassio. Here are not one but two villas built for William Montagu Scott McMurdo, one of the riviera's earliest British residents. The first (1875) is in an Anglo-Indian style with three tiers of ample porches; the second (1880) in a more opulent Eclectic style, with precious marbles inside and patterned brickwork and an Albisola majolica-clad dome outside. The buildings are set in a stunning botanical garden begun by the original owner and enriched with exotic species by Daniel Hanbury, son of Sir Thomas Hanbury of Mortola, who purchased the property in 1922. The 13 suites are spacious and elegant, and the service is impeccable. Hitchcock shot part of his first film, *The Pleasure Garden*, here in 1925, and the artist and writer Carlo Levi made some of his finest paintings on the grounds in the 1960s and 1970s. *Via Privata Montagu 9/1, T: 0182 646130 or 0182 646140, www. villadellapergola.com.*

ALBENGA (*map A, B2*)
€ **Torre Ceppolini.** This delightful property, somewhere between *hotel de charme*, B&B and private home, occupies the 12th-century tower and 13th-century townhouse of a once-powerful family in the heart of the old town, just a stone's throw from the cathedral and museums. The tall, narrow structure develops on five floors, so you should be prepared for stairs. Though the property faces Albenga's main street (the *decumanus maximus* of the ancient Roman town), the rooms are quiet and serene. *Via Medaglie d'Oro 25, T: 346 058 6804, www.torrecepollini.it.*

BORDIGHERA (*map A, A2*)
€€ **Villa Elisa.** A plunge into the Bordighera that was, this Belle-époque villa in the upper town has kept the atmosphere of a private home. The interior décor is elegant and serene, with an interesting mix of contemporary and antique furniture; the Mediterranean garden, with its olives, citrus trees and myriad flowers, offers a pool, sauna and a small playground for children. *Via Romana 70, T: 0184 261313, www.villaelisa.com.*

BORGOMARO (*map A, B2*)
€€ **Relais del Maro.** By the Torrente Maro, a tributary of the Impero, in Liguria's finest olive country, lies Borgomaro, a village of fewer than 1,000 inhabitants. Relais del Maro is a hotel, occupying several ancient houses in the village and has used traditional knowledge (and local artisans) in the restoration of its architectural spaces and the creation of its furnishings. Exposed stone and wood ceilings, beautiful fabrics and handcrafted furniture are just a few of the hallmarks of this unusual

establishment, set amidst the terraced hills 15km (20mins) inland from Imperia. *Via Guglieri 1, T: 0183 54350, www.relaisdelmaro.it.*

CERVO (*map A, B2*)

€ Le Notti Mediterranee. This delightful little B&B is right in the centre of the village. You have walk in with your bags (it's only a few metres from the town gate; the streets of Cervo are too narrow for cars), but the bad news ends here. Rooms are cosy and comfortable, history is all around you, and the venues of the summer music festival are just one to five minutes away on foot. *Via Cavour 9, T: 348 333 6899, www.lenottimediterranee.com.*

GARLENDA

€€€ La Meridiana. ■ Garlenda is a small village in the hills above medieval Albenga (*map A, B2*). It enjoys splendid views of the coast, in one direction, and the forested mountains separating Liguria from Piedmont in the other. The hotel is a luxurious country house surrounded by gardens, with an excellent restaurant. Peace and quiet rule, here, though the coastal resorts are just half an hour away by car. *Via ai Castelli, T: 0182 580271, www. lameridianaresort.com.*

IMPERIA (*map A, B2*)

€€ Relais San Damian. In an outstanding location high in the hills above Imperia, with broad views over the countryside to the sea, San Damian is a working farm as well as an elegant and relaxing place to stay. Bedrooms are large, comfortable and colourful, and furnished with rustic antiques. There is a cool, arcaded veranda on stout brick piers overlooking the palm-shaded garden, and a horizon pool from which you can spot Saracen invaders long before they reach the shore. All

the jams and preserves at the breakfast buffet are homemade, and the fruit and vegetables are garden/orchard-grown. *Strada Vasia 47, T: 0183 280309, www. san-damian.com.*

NOLI (*map A, C2*)

€€ Palazzo Vescovile. The former palace of the bishops of Noli (1239–1820), this beautiful hotel stands on a headland that can reached from the historic city centre by winding sreets or by lift. Common areas and guest rooms are warm and inviting, and there are fresco fragments scattered here and there in the rooms. The **Vescovado restaurant** ■ is one of the finest in Liguria and should be seriously considered by all with a penchant for fine food; it occupies beautifully furnished 15th-century rooms, and there is summer seating on a terrace overlooking the sea. *Piazzale Rosselli/ Viale Marconi. T: 019 749 9059, www. hotelvescovado.it.*

PIGNA (*map A, A1*)

€ Casa Rosa. Pigna is very much off the beaten track, buried deep in the the mountains of western Liguria near the French border, the Parco Naturale Regionale delle Alpi Ligure and the Ligurian High Trail. Here you'll find peace, quiet and authenticity, not only in the architecture of this lovingly restored 17th-century village house, but also in the style with which it is managed. Needless to say, if you come this far you should bring your hiking boots, and stay more than one night. *Corso De Sonnaz 35, T: 347 522 7119, www.bebcasarosa.com.*

SAN REMO (*map A, A2*)

€€€ Royal Hotel. With a vast and majestic Art-Nouveau façade overlooking the sea, a cool shady park and a salt-water swimming pool designed by the architect Gio Ponti, this is one of the Riviera's grandest grand hotels. Established in 1872, it has a guest book that includes aristocrats (Elisabeth of Austria, kings Farouk of Egypt and Hassan II of Morocco, Queen Rania of Jordan) artists (Pietro Mascagni) and scientists (Albert Sabin). Rebuilt after the Second World War, when the Fiori di Murano restaurant was added, it continues to offer guests the service of times gone by. *Corso Imperatrice 80, T: 0184 5391, www.royalhotelsanremo.com.*

VENTIMIGLIA (*map A, A2*)
€€ Baia Beniamin. Five nicely furnished rooms on a luxuriant little bay, with garden. *Corso Europa 63. T: 0184 38002, www.baiabeniamin.it.*

WHERE TO EAT ON THE RIVIERA DI PONENTE

ALASSIO (*map A, B2*)
€€€ Il Palma. Not a restaurant, a school of thought with food as its medium. The philosophy is there, but it's imperceptible: all you see/taste/smell are the most delicious creative interpretations of traditional Ligurian recipes imaginable, served in a refined setting in the heart of the old town. *Via Cavour 5, T: 0182 640314, www.ilpalma.com.*

€€ Caffè Pasticceria Balzola. Balzola is credited for two invaluable inventions: the delicious *Baci d'Alassio* (whose recipe was patented in 1919 by Rinaldo Balzola, later pastry chef of the kings of Italy) and the *caffè concerto*, where the little cream-filled biscuits could be munched while listening to live performances by the likes of Beniamino Gigli. Alassio's English residents met in the Venetian Revival interior, as did visiting intellectuals: Maxim Gorky, Gabriele D'Annunzio and Eleanora Duse were all clients, it seems. *Piazza Matteotti 26, T: 0182 640209, www.balzola1902.com.*

ALBISOLA SUPERIORE (*map A, D2*)
€€ U Fundegu. Family-run restaurant in a beautiful historic building, specialising in traditional Ligurian cuisine. Open evenings only May–August; open for lunch and dinner Sept–April daily except Weds. *Via Spotorno 87, T: 019 528 2286, www.ufundegu.it.*

ARMA DI TAGGIA (*map A, A2*)
€€ La Conchiglia. This is one of the finest places on the coast, famous for its outstanding regional cuisine, especially fish; flavours are delicate and carefully balanced, and presentation is flawless. The seaside location is very good, and there is outside seating in summer. *Lungomare 33, T: 0184 43169, www.laconchigliaristorante.eu.*

BORDIGHERA (*map A, A2*)
€ La Via Romana. This excellent fish restaurant occupies a Liberty villa from the early years of the 20th century. The cooking is as exuberant as the architecture, drawing on the traditions of the entire Mediterranean region. *Via Romana 57, T: 0184 266681, www.descurundu.it/viaromana.htm.*

€ Magiargè. This simple *osteria* offering delicious local cooking and great wines was one of the driving forces behind the 'renaissance' of Bordighiera Alta, the old town on the hill above the yacht harbour. The spearhead of a gourmet movement involving several local restaurants (and, of course, their clients), it offers excellent value for money. *Piazza Giacomo Viale, T: 0184 262946, www. magiarge.it.*

BORGO VEREZZI (*map A, C2*)

€€ **Da Casetta.** A warm family-run place in a lovely historic building, this establishment is known for its regional delicacies (if you haven't had the famous local snails, *lumache alla verezzina*, this is the place to try them). The ambience is rustic (the bedrock on which the house is built intrudes into the dining room), but the cuisine is refined. *Piazza San Pietro 12, T: 019 610166.*

CERVO (*map A, B2*)

€€ **Serafino.** Where tradition is concerned Serafino (the man) is the Rock of Gibraltar: only fish (prawns, shellfish) from *his* coast are served here, and every one has to pass muster before entering the kitchen. Serafino (the restaurant) is an unpretentious place opening onto a vaulted lane of the old town, with a panoramic terrace for summer; there are also a few simple rooms. *Via Matteotti 8, T: 0183 408185, www.daserafino.com.*

€ **Bellavista.** This simple place is famous for its homemade pasta, its delicate fish dishes, and its absolutely amazing historic collection of ships in bottles, a passion of the founder, a merchant-marine captain who spent much of his career in the treacherous waters off Cape Horn. The restaurant is right across the square from the town's upper gate and commands marvellous views. There are rooms, all perfectly comfortable and some with the same outstanding view. *Piazza Castello 2. T: 0183 408094, www.bellavistacervo.com.*

IMPERIA (*map A, B2*)

€€ **Lanterna Blu.** A truly outstanding seafood restaurant by the marina, known for its refined atmosphere, its excellent French and Italian wines, and fish so fresh they seem to have jumped out of the water and into the pan. *Via Scarincio 32 (Porto Maurizio, Borgo Marina) T: 0183 63859, www. lanternablu.it.*

€ **Caffè Piccardo.** The history of Piccardo reads like a novel. The café had been open just three years when, in 1908, the young Mussolini had his face slapped by the proprietor after making an impudent remark. In 1946 the cyclist Fausto Coppi, having a 14-minute advantage in the Milan–San Remo bicycle race, stopped in for a quick coffee, then got back on his bike and rode on to win. Composer Luciano Berio, writer Italo Calvino, and President of the Republic Sandro Pertini are among the café's famous customers; today you'll find people from all walks of life flocking to Piccardo for its delicious *stroscia*, a sweet dry focaccia made with lemon zest, vermouth and abundant local olive oil. *Piazza Dante 2, T: 0183 293696, caffepiccardo.wordpress.com.*

NOLI (*map A, C2*)

For the Vescovado restaurant, see p. 57.

SAN REMO (*map A, A2*)

€€ **Impekabile.** This new bar and grill, opened on the bicycle and pedestrian trail at Bussana in the summer of 2014, is already the trendiest place in town. The architecture is pointedly contemporary, as is the food and the way it is presented. The name sets the bar rather high, but for the time being the four founders are fulfilling their promise. *Pista Ciclabile del Parco Costiero e della Riviera Dei Fiori km13, T: 348 8762060, www.impekabile.com.*

€€€ **Le Vie del Sale.** Established in 2012, this is already one of the region's best restaurants, serving delicious local specialities, especially fish, and dishes from the tradition of Piedmont. *Lungomare Trento e Trieste 23, T: 0184 189 3343, www.ristoranteleviedelsale.it.* €€ **Osteria del Marinaio.** This small, friendly restaurant in the heart of San Remo has a long-standing reputation for good seafood and other local specialties. And not without reason: everything is prepared and presented with the greatest care, and the service is outstanding. *Via Gaudio 28, T: 0184 840387, osteriamarinaio.altervista.org.*

SAVONA (*map A, C2*)
€€ **Angolo dei Papi.** Situated on the corner between Palazzo della Rovere and the Cappella Sistina, this excellent traditional restaurant makes what may well be the best *cappon magro* in Liguria. It's made on the spot, of course, which means you'll want an *antipasto* to munch on while you're waiting. *Vico Del Marmo, 10, T: 019 854263, www.langolodeipapi.eu.*

VENTIMIGLIA (*map A, A2*)
€€€ **Balzi Rossi.** This is the first gourmet restaurant you encounter in Liguria—or the last, depending on which way you're going. It's located so close to the border that breadcrumbs from your table fall in France. It's rightly known for its very fine regional cuisine and its beautiful views of sea and coast, particularly from the summer terrace. It may, in fact, be a bit too famous, drawing clients whose spending capacity exceeds their other qualities. *Via Balzi Rossi 2, T: 0184 38132, www.ristorantebalzirossi.com.*
€ **Bookaffè.** Really just a café with kitchen—but a good one. There *are* books, true and faux (that is, laser-printed on wall and floor surfaces). As well as WiFi, which means you can have a nice light meal or snack (indoors or out) and browse the web between trains, the station being just around the corner. *Via Hanbury 2c, T: 347 960 4577.*

The Riviera di Levante

The Riviera di Levante has long been a major tourist destination, thanks to its natural beauty, its artistic heritage and its mild climate, the result of the influence of the sea and the protection its mountains and hills provide from the cold winds of northern Italy. The coast south and east of Genoa, from Nervi to Camogli, is rather emphatically called the Bay of Paradise. Its air of luxury is due to the fact that property ownership is shared by seasonal visitors from Milan, Turin and elsewhere in Italy and Europe, and wealthy residents who feel the snail-paced commute to and from Genoa is an acceptable trade-off for life in such a 'heavenly' spot. The town of Recco (*map B, B2*) was badly damaged by bombs in the Second World War, making it a rather anonymous, modern place you today, but home to some good restaurants. Next comes the Portofino peninsula, with the well-known resort of aristocrats and celebrities, and the very beautiful former fishing town of Santa Margherita Ligure. The lovely Golfo di Tigullio extends between Rapallo and Sestri Levante, a quiet and beautiful place huddled between two bays. Beyond, the coast becomes higher and more dramatic—qualities it will retain all the way to the Gulf of La Spezia, at Liguria's eastern tip, with Portovenere and Lerici. Here, between Sestri and La Spezia, is the most famous stretch of coast in northern Italy, the Cinque Terre.

RIVIERA DI LEVANTE TRIVIA

- In 1852 Niccolò Schiaffino of Camogli founded the first insurance company, the Mutua Assicurazione Marittima, specifically designed to pay damages in the event that a ship sank.
- In 1856 more ships were registered in Camogli (580) than in Hamburg.
- In the 1950s the film stars were so numerous at Portofino, it was nicknamed Hollywood by the Sea.
- Sciacchetrà may be the only Italian wine with a Hebrew name (from *shakar*, to make drunk). The wine was so precious it was reserved by Genoese merchants as a gift to partners and clients, some of whom apparently appreciated it highly.

THE PORTOFINO PENINSULA

The beautiful, green Portofino peninsula rises proudly at the southern end of the

Golfo del Paradiso. Once threatened by real-estate development, the promontory came under environmental protection astonishingly early, in 1935. Today it is a nature reserve administered by the Region of Liguria and includes the municipalities of Camogli, Portofino and Santa Margherita Ligure. With 80km of marked trails on just over 1500 hectares of land, it is a true paradise for walkers. Walks are well signed with a variety of waymarks (dots, lozenges) and a detailed trail map is available at the park office (*Viale Rainusso 1, Santa Margherita Ligure; open weekdays 9–12.30; see www.parcoportofino.it*). Maps are also to be found in bookshops and at the kiosk opposite the bus terminus in Portofino.

CAMOGLI

Set on the west side of the Portofino peninsula, Camogli (*map B, B2*) is a picturesque little fishing port descending steeply to a rocky shore. It was famous for its merchant ships in the days of sail, its fleet having played a prominent part in the naval wars of Napoleon, of Louis-Philippe, and in the Crimea, where it successfully defied a Russian blockade to send supplies to Anglo-French troops. It is interesting for its architecture, with unusually tall, colourful houses lining the seafront.

Camogli's only extant fortification, the **Castello della Dragonara**, stands on a rocky headland in the oldest part of the town. It is a small but tough-looking four-square fortress with three watchtowers originally constructed in 1130, as a refuge from Saracen incursions, and rebuilt several times before being demilitarised in 1560. It now holds a little multimedia presentation of the town's history and its socio-economic ties to the sea. The adjacent church of **Santa Maria Assunta**, founded in the 12th century but rebuilt and enlarged several times over the following centuries, has a Neoclassical front overlooking a pretty little 17th-century square with a black-and-white inlaid cobblestone pavement. The stern façade conceals a stunning display of marble, statuary and gilded stucco inside, with locally painted frescoes on the ceiling and a *Deposition* by Luca Cambiaso in the sacristy.

There is only one museum in Camogli, and in its quaint, old-fashioned way it's a real treat. No one who has ever built a ship model—or knows someone who has built one—will want to miss the **Museo Marinaro** (*Via Gio Bono Ferrari 41; steps opposite Camogli–San Fruttuso railway station; open Mon, Thur and Fri 9–12; Wed, Sat and Sun 9–12 & 3–6; www.museomarinaro.it*), which tells the 300-year story of Camogli's tall ships and their crews. Everything you see here was donated by the city's seafaring families and the museum is staffed by volunteers. Paintings, photographs, models and documents represent just a few of the 3000 sailing ships that the *camogliesi* owned and operated between the Napoleonic Wars and World War I. For those who are not up on their sailing ship classifications, it will be useful to know that a *brigantino* (brig) is a slender and manageable, two-masted square-rigged ship typically having an additional lower fore-and-aft sail on the gaff and a boom to the mainmast; it is relatively small (100–300 tonnes). A *brigantino a palo* (barque) is a medium-sized sailing ship, typically with three masts, in which the foremast and mainmast are square-rigged and the mizzenmast is rigged fore and aft; common in the 16th–18th centuries, it is larger than a brig (600–2000 tonnes).

A *goletta* (schooner) is a gaff-rigged sailing ship with a bowsprit and two or more masts, typically with the foremast smaller than the mainmast. A treasure of the museum is the chronometer from the *Narcissus*, the ship immortalised in literature by Joseph Conrad.

WALKS FROM CAMOGLI

From Camogli a pretty walk leads south to San Rocco, the Romanesque church of San Nicolò, and (*1hr 15mins*) **Punta Chiappa**, a stony promontory where the view is remarkable for the ever-changing colours of the sea. A rough-hewn altar on the point reproduces in mosaic a graffito found at San Nicolò. Other trails lead to the **Monte di Portofino** (*1hr 30mins; strenuous*) and to **San Fruttuoso** (*2hrs; moderate*). If you choose to walk to San Fruttuoso, be sure to take the high trail, as the low one involves some tricky rock-climbing.

Beyond San Rocco the relatively easy walk ascends gently along the western slope of the Monte di Portofino to the hamlet of **La Mortola**, with its *trompe l'oeil* house façades, amidst natural vegetation and farmland, offering a variety of good views over the Golfo del Paradiso to Genoa and beyond. The uncultivated areas here include authentic Mediterranean forests of holm oak, hornbeam and manna ash (the Aleppo pines further up the slope are part of a reforestation scheme); in the water below you can see dark green 'meadows' of the seagrass *poseidonia*, a good indicator of ecosystem integrity. Beyond La Mortola the olive trees are no longer tended, and the landscape becomes increasingly wild as you approach Toca, 450m above the Cala dell'Oro, the little bay to the west of San Fruttuoso. The trail climbs to **Pietra Stretta**, offering magnificent views, before descending along the ridge line between the twin coves of Cala dell'Oro and San Fruttuso, first amidst invasive bracken and bramble that have replaced the Mediterranean maquis destroyed by wildfire, then through cool, shady forest to San Fruttuoso. The trail continues, via Olmi, to Portofino (*1hr 30mins; easy*).

SAN FRUTTUOSO DI CAPODIMONTE

This former Benedictine abbey and its picturesque little hamlet lies right on the sea in a rocky inlet of a lovely bay surrounded by wooded hills. It can be reached by boat or on foot, but not by road. There are cafés and snack bars on the bay.

Getting to San Fruttuoso

The walking map of the Portofino peninsula marks easy-to-follow trails to San Fruttuoso from Camogli, Portofino and Santa Margherita. Boats run to San Fruttuoso from Camogli, Portofino, Santa Margherita Ligure, Rapallo, Sestri Levante, Recco, Lavagna, Chiavari and Genoa. Services run all year round but are much less frequent in winter. For timetables from Recco and Camogli, see www.golfoparadiso.it; from Portofino and Santa Margherita, see www.traghettiportofino.it; from Genoa, see www.battellierigenova.it. Timetables are also posted at the harbours, including at San Fruttuoso.

THE ABBEY

The abbey of San Fruttuoso (*open daily except Mon, June–early Sept 10–5.45; March, late Sept and Oct 10–4.45; April–May 10–4.45; Nov–Feb 10–3.45; for more details, see www.visitfai.it/sanfruttuoso*) is a property of the Fondo per l'Ambiente Italiana (FAI), a national conservation trust, and was restored on their initiative in the late 20th century.

An abbey was founded here beside an abundant spring before the 10th century and was of great importance in the 11th and 12th centuries. It was reconstructed by the Doria in the 13th century, but was deserted by the Benedictines in 1467. It survived under Doria patronage until 1885, after which the buildings were taken over by fishermen and severely damaged by the sea in 1915. They were donated by the Doria Pamphilj family to the FAI in 1983, and restored after 1989.

The abbey and church are supported on large vaulted arches. The upper cloister was built in the 12th century and restored in the 16th (it includes Roman and medieval capitals). In the 13th-century part of the abbey you can see 13th- and 14th-century ceramics found during the excavations and other material documenting the abbey, its times, and monastic life. The lower cloister and church, with an unusual dome, date in part from the 10th century. The 13th-century crypt contains Doria tombs in white marble and grey Phrygian stone.

The grey square Torre Doria was erected on the point in 1561 as a defence against pirates. The tower is turned out so two sides face the sea; both bearing the crest of the Doria family, and other decorations are visible on the frames, and on the shelves.

A bronze statue of Christ with arms outstretched *Christ of the Abyss*, by Guido Galletti (1954), stands offshore, eight fathoms down, as protector of all those who work beneath the sea. A torchlight Mass is held in summer in memory of the drowned.

PORTOFINO

Once a romantic fishing village with pretty houses, Portofino (*map B, B2*) is now an exclusive resort in a beautiful position, partly on a small wooded headland, and partly in a little bay that has offered a safe anchorage to boats since Roman times. Today *Forbes* lists it among the five most expensive places to moor your yacht (at the time of writing USD 3,335/night). Although it can be horribly overcrowded in high season (the access road is actually closed on summer weekends), for most of the year Portofino is a wonderful place to wander.

According to Pliny the Elder, Portofino was founded during the Roman Empire under the name of *Portus Delphini* due to the large population of dolphins in the Gulf of Tigullio.

The parish church, **Divo Martino**, dedicated to St Martin of Tours, who lived for a time on the Isle of Gallinara and may have been one of the first visitors here, is located in the oldest part of Portofino. It was built in the Lombard Romanesque style in the 12th century but has been altered several times since. The richly decorated interior holds a wooden *Deposition* by Anton Maria Maragliano.

The little church of **San Giorgio**, overlooking the harbour, is said to hold the relics of its namesake—patron saint of Portofino and protector of Genoese mariners, brought from the Holy Land by returning Crusaders. The saint's heraldic symbol, a red cross on a white field, was taken as the emblem of the Genoese Republic, of armed pilgrims to the Holy Land (who came to be known as Crusaders precisely because of this insignia) and, after the 12th century, by England, initially as a sign to Mediterranean pirates that its ships sailed under the protection of the Genoese fleet. Sadly, this building is a modern reconstruction: the original was levelled by a direct bomb hit in the Second World War.

On the harbour below San Giorgio, and stretching up the hillside, is the little **Museo del Parco** (*www.museodiportofino.it*), a sculpture garden with works by Pomodoro, Messina and other modern Italian masters.

CASTELLO BROWN AND PUNTA DEL CAPO

The scenic fortress of St George, later renamed **Castello Brown** after Montague Yeats Brown, the British Consul in Genoa who owned it in the late 19th century, is built on Roman foundations. Surrounded by walls, it has a tower and a central keep. The castle was a possession of the Benedictines of San Fruttuoso in the 11th century, then of Rapallo, and from the 15th century, of the Genoese, who sold it to Brown in 1867. Later owned by Alfons von Mumm (the champagne maker), it now belongs to the municipality of Portofino, which uses it for special events. It is also open for visits (*www.castellobrown.com*).

The castle comes with a story, which can still be heard in the piazzetta's open-air cafés on warm summer evenings. It appears that Von Mumm's Scottish widow, Jeannie Mackay-Watt, saved Portofino from destruction by the retreating Nazis by persuading the garrison commander not to set off the mines that had been laid in the village and its harbour: Castello Brown, too, had been mined, but the elderly, reclusive Jeannie refused to leave it as ordered; the young commander, navy lieutenant Ernst Reimers, sickened by the idea of creating yet another pointless victim, drove off without detonating the charges. His decision may have saved his own life as well as Jeannie's as, when later captured and tried for war crimes, his sentence acknowledged his disobedience of this last command. It is not clear how much Reimers knew of another incident remembered in Portofino, in which 22 political prisoners were 'secretly' executed at the little beach of Olivetta by Italian Fascists loyal to the Salò Republic and their German *camerati*. The victims were shot at night and their bodies tied together, weighted and cast into the sea.

The pathway by the castle continues to the **Punta del Capo** (*15mins*) with a lighthouse and a small café serving refreshments (including home-made ice cream) in summer. It is the most pleasant walk in Portofino and one everyone can do, as the pathway is paved and more or less level.

THE INTERNATIONAL ELITE AT PORTOFINO

La Gritta American Bar, on the waterfront at Portofino, is adorned inside with photographs of Rex Harrison and other leading lights of yore. Ask the barman, as he mixes your Campari soda, what the tiny resort is like in summer, and he throws up his hands: 'Too much people, too much money, too much, too much!'

The historic archives of the Genoa press agency Publifoto (*www.publifoto. net*) has hundreds of images of 'Liguria as it was', including a complete set of snapshots of Portofino's VIP visitors. Do a keyword search for 'Portofino' and you will see Rex Harrison (in 1954, with Lilli Palmer), as well as the Duke and Duchess of Windsor (1952 and 1955), Ingrid Bergman (1952), Clark Gable (1953), Jayne Mansfield (1953), Greta Garbo (1953), Vivien Leigh (1954), Alan Ladd (1954), Ava Gardner, Lauren Bacall and Humphrey Bogart (here for the filming of Joseph L. Mankiewicz's *La Contessa Scalza* in 1954), Aristotle Onassis (1955), Rex Harrison again, this time with Kay Kendall (1958), Virna Lisi (1959), Elizabeth Taylor (1959), James Stewart (1960), Raymond Burr (1960), Glenn Ford (1962), Princess Soraya (1961), Juan Carlos of Spain and Princess Sophia (on their honeymoon, 1962) and Gregory Peck (1971).

ABBAZIA DELLA CERVARA
On the coast between Portofino and Santa Margherita Ligure a short way north of the small, secluded bay of Paraggi (*map B, B2*), is the former 14th-century abbey of La Cervara, where Francis I of France was held prisoner after the Battle of Pavia (1525) and where Gregory XI rested on the return of the papacy from Avignon to Rome (1377). The complex was constructed in 1361 on a commission from Ottone Lanfranco, chaplain of the church of Santo Stefano di Genova, in honour of St Jerome. In 1420 the Benedictines acquired the property and in 1546 fortified it against the incursions of Saracen pirates. Declared a national monument in 1912, it has been painstakingly restored as a privately-owned events venue and can be visited by appointment (*March–Oct 1st and 3rd Sun of the month, tours starting at 10, 11 and 12, free phone 800 65 21 10, www.cervara.it*). The interiors are impeccably furnished and the former kitchen garden of the monks has been transformed into a gorgeous Renaissance Revival park (Grandi Giardini Italiani prize, 2012).

SANTA MARGHERITA LIGURE

Probably the best base for exploring the Portofino peninsula without paying the exorbitant prices of its namesake is Santa Margherita Ligure (*map B, B2*), a fishing village that became a seaside resort at the end of the 19th century, growing in the 20th to become one of the most popular destinations on the riviera.

The discovery of a 3rd-century ad cinerary urn with a Latin inscription (now preserved in the basilica of Nostra Signora della Rosa) supports the the otherwise unproven hypothesis that there was a settlement here in Roman times. A fishing village on this spot was destroyed several times in the Middle Ages, first by Rothair's Lombards and then by the Saracens, before becoming a fief of the Fieschi family of Genoa in 1229. The village's two distinct (and rival) neighbourhoods were united under the French and granted municipal status under the Savoy kings, Vittorio Emanuele II formally acknowledging the name Santa Margherita in 1863. In the last quarter of the 19th century the construction of the railway and the carriage road to Portofino made tourism, rather than fishing, Santa Margherita's chief source of wealth.

EXPLORING SANTA MARGHERITA

The 17th-century **Villa Durazzo** stands at the top of the town, surrounded by a luxuriant park. Designed in 1678 by Galeazzo Alessi as a summer residence of the Durazzo family (and sold in 1821 to the Centurione), its dark red walls contrast nicely with the green park, especially lush in spring (*open daily, summer 9–7, winter 9–5; www.villadurazzo.it*). The palace's monumental garden entrance is preceded by a lovely rissëu cobblestone terrace by Giovanni Franceschetti, decorated with 17th- and 18th-century allegorical statues and enjoying fine vistas of the town and the Golfo di Tigullio. The interior (*open summer 9–1 & 2.30–6.30, winter 9–1 & 2–5*) holds a mildly interesting collection of furniture and paintings, which is shown when the villa is not being used for exhibitions or events.

The approach to Villa Durazzo from the waterfront (there is another entrance from Via Principi Centurione, in the centre of town) climbs past the 17th-century collegiate church of **San Giacomo di Corte**, with a spectacular Baroque façade and a cycle of 19th-century frescoes by Nicolò Barbarino within. At the bottom of the steps is the little oratory of **Sant'Erasmo**, fronted by another fine cobbled pavement and with a fine collection of sailors' ex-votos inside. Directly below the church is the **fish market**, where sailors still come to sell their daily catch.

Santa Margherita's diminutive **castle**, on a cobbled slope just above the waterfront, was built after 1550 to defend the town from Saracen incursions, which were particularly frequent in in the 16th century. Like the villa, it is now used for exhibitions and cultural events. Behind it, with a modern porch adorned with mosaics, is the church of the **Cappuccini**, which holds a revered 13th-century statue of the *Madonna Enthroned*.

RISSËU

This peculiarly Genoese form of cobblestone paving, which was enormously fashionable in the 17th and 18th centuries, may be inspired by Graeco-Roman mosaics the Republic's mariners encountered as they sailed the Mediterranean—or, according to another theory, by the Ligurian custom of composing patterns of flower petals on the streets for the late-spring feast of Corpus Christi. The bonding medium is lime mortar and porcelain powder; the water-smoothed pebbles that make up the design are chosen for their size and colour: black, white and occasionally red. The word is Genoese dialect for 'pebble' and may derive from the French *ruisseau*, a stream or brook. Beautiful *rissëu* pavements can be seen throughout Liguria.

The waterfront and the shopping streets leading from the square outside the imposing Baroque basilica of **Nostra Signora della Rosa** (where the Roman funerary urn is preserved) are well worth a wander. Don't miss the **fresh pasta shop** on Via Cavour/Corso Matteotti, with its wonderful old machines.

AROUND SANTA MARGHERITA

The church at **San Michele di Pagana** (*map B, B2*), a tiny village on the seaward side of the road from Santa Margherita to Rapallo (you can walk there from Santa

Margherita, but take care, as the road is narrow and busy), has a fine *Crucifixion* by Van Dyck, who stayed here in 1621–4. Nearby, in a large park, is the Villa Spinola or Villa del Trattato, where the Treaty of Rapallo between Italy and the former Yugoslavia was signed in 1920. The 16th-century Torre di Punta Pagana, another defensive tower, stands amidst tall pines at the seaward end of the park. Inland from Santa Margherita is **San Lorenzo della Costa**, where the church preserves the late 15th-century *Triptych of St Andrew*, by a Flemish artist.

RAPALLO

Rapallo (*map B, B2*) gives its name to *rapallizzazione*, which translates loosely as 'pouring too much concrete into too small an area'. It is the best known holiday resort on the Riviera di Levante and was the first, historically, to suffer from overdevelopment. Although the lovely surroundings, which used to be the main attraction of Rapallo, have been carpeted with anonymous residential architecture and the mole of the new yacht basin has blocked the view out to sea, you can still spend a pleasant morning or afternoon here. The writers Max Beerbohm (1872–1956) and Ezra Pound (1885–1972) both had homes in Rapallo.

The **castle**, on a rock in the harbour reached by a causeway, was built in 1546 after the city had been looted and many of its inhabitants abducted by the Turkish corsair Dragut. It was restored at the end of the 20th century as an exhibition centre but is most famous for its role in the annual pyrotechnic display for the feast of the Madonna di Montallegro (2–3 July), when fireworks cascade from the ramparts and countless lanterns (*lumetti*) float in the harbour waters.

The shrine of **Nostra Signora di Montallegro**, situated on a hill 612m above sea level and offering breathtaking views of the entire Gulf of Tigullio, can be reached on foot (by a stony *creuza* starting from the church of San Francesco, in 1hr 30mins), or by a spectacular cable car (from Piazzale Solari, 7mins). The Virgin Mary appeared to a peasant here on the night of 2nd July 1557, leaving a small (15cm by 18cm) icon as a testimony of her visit. The farmer took the painting into the city for safekeeping, but by the next morning it had returned to the point where Mary had made her appearance and where a cool spring had begun to flow. The interior of the shrine holds the icon (in an 18th-century case) and an amazing number of votive offerings.

The former convent of the Poor Clares (Piazzale Josemaria Escriva) now houses the **Museo Attilio e Cleofe Gaffoglio** (*open June–Sept Wed, Fri and Sat 3–6, Thur 10–12, Sun and holidays 3–5; July and Aug Wed, Fri and Sat 10–12, Thur, Sun and holidays 5–7*) featuring the Gaffoglio collection of decorative arts. Here are more than 300 examples of 14th–20th-century porcelain, pottery, silver and ivories, and a small group of paintings and sculptures, mainly from the 19th and early 20th centuries.

The 19th-century **Villa Tigullio**, surrounded by the beautiful Parco Casale on the eastern waterfront by the breakwater, is home to the Museo del Merletto (*open summer Wed, Fri and Sat 4–7, Thur 10–12, Sun and holidays 5–7; winter Wed, Fri and Sat 3–6, Thur 10–12, Sun and holidays 3–5*). This is an extraordinary museum dedicated wholly to bobbin lace, which has been made on this coast since the 16th century; the collection includes adults' and children's clothing and accessories, household linens and decorator items, sketches and bobbins, mainly from the archives of the Zennaro firm, which made lace in Rapallo from 1908–68. The same building holds Rapallo's Biblioteca Internazionale, founded in 1957 by a group of women of different nationalities: the library features a fine collection of historic travel guides from the 19th century onwards (including L. Russell Muirhead's 1956 *Blue Guide Short Guide to London*).

Close to the port, spanning the road that leads out of Rapallo towards Santa Margherita, is a single-arched bridge named **Ponte di Annibale**, from the fanciful notion that it was built by Hannibal during the Punic Wars.

CHIAVARI

Chiavari (*map B, B2*) is a large but pleasant place with an arcaded old main street and a sandy beach. Here Garibaldi, on his arrival in exile from the south, was arrested on 6th Sept 1849 'in the most polite and friendly manner possible', because his forebears came from the town. Two other Risorgimento heroes, Nino Bixio and Giuseppe Mazzini, also descended from old Chiavari families. Chiavari has a fine old historic café.

SESTRI LEVANTE & THE CINQUE TERRE

Sestri Levante (*map B, B2*), in a delightful position at the base of the peninsula of Isola (once an island), is a summer resort with a vaguely aristocratic air; in addition to its own merits (two sandy beaches and some of the finest gourmet food in the region) it is an excellent starting point for day trips to the Cinque Terre.

From Piazza Matteotti, with the 17th-century parish church, a street ascends to the restored Romanesque church of **San Nicolò dell'Isola**, dating originally from 1151. This is one of the best preserved examples of Romanesque architecture on the riviera, and its quiet, scenic location makes it a wonderful place for a stroll. Continuing up the hill you reach the **Villa Gualino**, now a hotel, rebuilt with antique materials (1925) on Genoese foundations, with a magnificent park, at the end of the peninsula. Guglielmo Marconi carried out his first experiments in short-wave radio transmission from the tower here, but to see it you have to buy your way onto the grounds (for example, by ordering a drink at the bar).

At the foot of the hill, on the little bay aptly called the Baia del Silenzio, is the **Galleria Rizzi** (*Via Cappuccini 8, open May–Oct Sun 10–1, Wed 4–7, Fri and Sat 9.30–11.30pm, www.galleriarizzi.com*), the early 20th-century house museum of art collector Marcello Rizzi, with a modest collection of 15th–18th-century paintings and sculpture from Liguria, Lombardy, Emilia Romagna, the Veneto and Tuscany.

In an elevated position overlooking the Baia del Silenzio is the 17th-century **Convento dei Cappuccini**, where the humble wooden altars in the church were crafted by the monks themselves. The Dominican Convento dell'Annunziata, across the bay, is now a meeting and teaching centre of the Fondazione Mediterraneo, an information sciences research organisation.

In the central **Piazza Bo** stands the *Vela per Colombo*, one of Gio Pomodoro's last works, bearing a verse of poet Mario Luzi (1914–2005), '*Quale viaggio ti hanno dato i venti...*' (What a journey have the winds given you...), suggesting that our free will is, perhaps, imperfect.

Sestri was the preferred place for Genoese aristocrats to build their summer houses, and no town in Liguria other than Genoa has more **patrician palaces**. Among the best in the town centre are Palazzo Durazzo Pallavicini (now the Town Hall) on Piazza Matteotti; Palazzo Fascie (now the municipal library and museum) at Corso Colombo 50; Villa Balbi (formerly Brignole, now a hotel with fine garden) at Viale Rimembranza 1; Palazzo Negrotto Cambiaso on the west shore of the Baia del Silenzio.

THE CINQUE TERRE

'A rocky, austere landscape, similar to Calabria's harshest, the refuge of fishermen and farmers living meagrely on an ever-smaller shred of beach, the naked and solemn frame of one of the most primitive lifestyles in Italy.' This is how Eugenio Montale described the coast of the Cinque Terre (*map B, C3*), the steepest and roughest in all Liguria. The area takes its name from the five little medieval villages—Monterosso al Mare, Vernazza, Corniglia, Manarola and Riomaggiore—that were accessible only by sea before the advent in 1874 of the railway, which tunnels through the rocky coast. By car they can be reached only along winding, steep inland roads.

From Montale's words one might expect to find a wilderness landscape here, a place that appears to have been affected primarily by the forces of nature, where the imprint of human labour is substantially unnoticeable; a place that retains its primeval character, in contrast with those areas where man and his own works dominate the natural environment. Yet the sheer, vertical landscape of the Cinque Terre is anything but wild. It is deeply marked by centuries of hard human labour, which have transformed its precipitous cliffs into an immense hanging garden.

Tens of thousands of walkers are drawn every year by the Cinque Terre's perpendicular vineyards, whose terraces—called *cian* in dialect—are the most distinctive physical feature of this 'shred' of earth and its community of life. More than a landscape design, the system of *cian* is a landscape sculpture; it has been compared also to an immense, ingenious work of open-air architecture.

How, why and when a project of such vast proportions was conceived remains an unsolved mystery. Also unanswered is the question of why grapes, and grapes alone, are grown on the terraced mountainsides. Historic examples of specialised farming like this are anything but common, and the few there are, are all situated in places that are easier to access, to work and to exploit commercially. No one knows quite why the choice fell on such an inaccessible area: the nearest highways are far away, even today, and from the sea, the only harbour of any importance was, for centuries, the little port of Vernazza. It may never be determined if the Cinque Terre are a spontaneous, haphazard creation, or a carefully crafted masterpiece of environmental engineering (the stepped terraces help retain rainwater that would otherwise run straight into the sea). As documentary evidence is entirely lacking, historians can only form hypotheses. One of these is proposed in the historical essay below.

Whatever the case may be, the historic struggle between man and nature in the Cinque Terre is far from over. The particular lie of the land make the terraces behave like tesserae in a mosaic: if more than a few are lost, the whole composition will collapse. Obviously, if the lowermost terraces are not maintained, a landslide risk arises. But the same danger forms if the ridge-top terraces are not worked: dirt and stones can damage those below beyond repair, dragging the whole system downward. Clearly, to abandon the vineyards would spell catastrophe not just for agriculture, but for the ecological integrity of the whole area. Great amounts of labour are needed to maintain the vineyards and the infrastructure of drystone walls, footpaths and watercourses needed to support them. Sustainable agriculture here means physically holding the landscape together. The substantial problem exists also of providing adequate compensation for those who remain committed to this primitive way of managing the land.

In 1997 UNESCO acknowledged that the Ligurian coast between the Cinque Terre and Portovenere 'is a cultural landscape of great scenic and cultural value' where 'the layout and disposition of the small towns and the shaping of the surrounding landscape, overcoming the disadvantages of a steep, uneven terrain, encapsulate the continuous history of human settlement in this region over the past millennium', and added the area to the World Heritage List. Given the high social value of the work of local farmers, and the need to regulate the pressure exerted on the landscape by recreational visitors, the Cinque Terre were declared a national park (*www. parconazionale5terre.it*) in 1999. The park's jurisdiction also extends over the sea, which is particularly rich in marine life and borders on the International Cetacean Sanctuary in the waters between Genoa, Corsica and Nice.

Most of the trails in the Cinque Terre are former mule tracks winding over the great green spurs that separate one village from the next: if you decide to walk from village to village, you will have to climb from sea level to an elevation of 200 or 300m, then descend again. Exceptions are the seaside trails from Corniglia to Manarola and from Manarola to Riomaggiore, both of which are without significant elevation gains. The latter, called the 'Lovers' Trail', even has benches. The most scenic trails are those leading from Monterosso and Corniglia to Vernazza, and the magnificent, lofty trail from Corniglia to Manarola via Volastra (*see below for details*).

Many people who visit the Cinque Terre are too exhausted to explore the villages when they come down off the trail. This is a mistake. Each tiny place has its hidden surprises. As there are no great monuments of art or architecture here, it is *only* by nosing around that the villages' charm can be fully savoured.

Hiking the Cinque Terre and getting around

*Monterosso is the starting point of the **Sentiero Azzurro** (route SVA), which follows the old mule path connecting the five villages. Connecting trails lead up to the **Alta Via delle Cinque Terre** (route AV5T or No. 1), which runs high up among the terraced vineyards.*

*Although there are car parks in all the villages, they tend to fill up quickly, and the endless curves on the roads in make driving hazardous and tiring. It is much better to visit the Cinque Terre by **train**, so if you get tired, or the weather takes a sudden turn for the worse, you can return to your starting point quickly and safely. Cheap Regionali and Regionali Veloci trains run frequently from village to village in all seasons (all five villages have railway stations and it is about 5mins journey between each; journey time to Riomaggiore from Genoa Piazza Principe station is approx. 1hr 40mins, sometimes quicker). In summer, villages are also connected by a **boat service**, with boats also going west to Portofino and east to Portovenere and Lerici (for timetables, routes and fares, see www. navigazionegolfodeipoeti.it). Other boats link Vernazza and Monterosso with Camogli and Genoa (www.golfoparadiso.it). Boat trips around the Cinque Terre (and other excursions, including whale watching) are also organised (www. liguriaviamare.it).*

*   **Visitors' Centres** *at the Monterosso and Riomaggiore train stations, the two gateways to the park, sell the **Cinque Terre Card**, which gives access to the main hiking trails as well as discounts on maps, books and gifts and reduced admission to the museums of La Spezia. To walk from one village to the next takes between one and two hours. The SVA route, marked with red and white waymarks, touches upon all five villages: fit, experienced walkers can 'do' the Cinque Terre in about 5hrs this way, not counting village visits (which of course are highly recommended). If you want to walk just one trail, the high trail from Corniglia to Manarola via Volastra is by far the most rewarding.*

*   *The best times to go to the Cinque Terre are spring, when the wildflowers are in bloom, and autumn, when the grape leaves turn bright gold and red. Summer is unbearably hot (especially on the ascents), and winter's high winds and squalls can make the more exposed tracts dangerous. This is also when the park authorities do major maintenance work.*

*   *At the time of writing (July 2014), the Sentiero Azzurro was closed between Vernazza and Riomaggiore due to landslides. For information, maps and updates, see www.parconazionale5terre.it.*

HISTORY OF THE CINQUE TERRE

The development of agriculture on a scale large enough to affect the landscape of the Cinque Terre came relatively late by Italian standards, around the year 1000. Before that time the rugged, inaccessible coast was blanketed with forest, even during the Roman era, when adjoining districts such as the plain of the River Magra were extensively farmed. The earliest settlements, Monterosso and Vernazza, appear in historical records in the 11th century, and it is probably at this time that local residents began to develop agricultural practices sufficient to produce a change in the landscape. Over the course of the next two centuries Corniglia, Manarola and Riomaggiore grew up, in that order, as the notion of organising settlement in villages spread eastward. All five towns are thought to have been established by populations from the mountains' upper slopes, driven by the need for an outlet to the sea, which at that time was the only means of communication with the outside world. By the end of the 13th century the territory probably looked much as it does today, with five small villages huddled at the foot of the steep, terraced hills.

In the 14th century the establishment of a highly successful wine trade sparked a period of prosperity in the Cinque Terre that lasted at least until the early 16th century and almost certainly led to an increase of the terraced area at the expense of the natural vegetation. At this time the vineyards are thought to have covered just over 300 hectares (an area roughly equal to that under cultivation in the late 20th century). Then, towards the end of the 1500s, the wine market collapsed and the territory was cast into a deep depression that lasted two full centuries. Some farmers attempted to diversify their cultivations, planting mulberry trees and breeding silkworms, or replacing their vineyards with lemon groves (of which quite a few can still be seen around Monterosso), while continuing to grow olives and chestnuts as they had done before. But these crops were never produced in sufficient quantities to provide viable economic alternatives to viticulture. Revenues plummeted and the land was abandoned: the dry-stone walls came tumbling down, the soil became unstable, and precious humus was lost to the sea. The degradation was such that when the municipalities of Riomaggiore, Manarola and Corniglia approved Liguria's Napoleonic constitution, at the turn of the 18th century, they signed under the collective name of *Distretto delle Montagne Sterili* (District of the Sterile Mountains).

Towards the middle of the 19th century the wine market sprang back, allowing the economy of the Cinque Terre to recover and even to grow. Then in 1874 the Genoa–La Spezia railway was completed and for the first time in their history the inhabitants of this rugged coast were no longer isolated from the rest of the region. The new transport infrastructure gave the local economy a boost, and by the end of the century the population of the Cinque Terre had nearly doubled. But it was in the early 20th century that the Cinque Terre registered its greatest growth in population and in terraced area, which at its peak covered about 1400 hectares, of which 800 under the vine. The vineyards extended from sea level to an elevation of roughly 500m, and altogether the drystone walls that supported them measured an estimated 7000km.

After the Second World War farmers again began to leave the land and the natural vegetation invaded a large part of the plots they left behind, with inevitable consequences for the stability of the area. By 1980 the terraced area had returned to its 16th-century extent, though the landscape now had two new features: the railway and the road from Riomaggiore to Monterosso, built halfway up the mountainside in the 1960s. Thanks largely to these two additions, in the 21st century the landscape of the Cinque Terre has reversed its course once more, turning from degradation to conservation. The economic driver, now, is not the precious wines that are made here, but the way they are made, the human history of the Cinque Terre and the shaping influence that history has had on the natural environment.

MONTEROSSO AL MARE

The westernmost of the Cinque Terre, Monterosso (*map B, C3*) is clustered around an inlet enclosed by hills terraced with olive and lemon trees and, above all, grapevines. Possibly founded in the 11th century, Monterosso was a fief of the Obertenghi and De Passano families until the 13th century, when the five villages were taken over and fortified by the Republic of Genoa.

The oldest part of the village develops linearly along the Torrente Buranco, which has been paved over to form the main street. Here, overlooking the beach, the little church of San Giovanni Battista has a 14th-century façade with black-and-white stonework, a rose window in finely worked white marble, and a Gothic doorway with an 18th-century fresco of the *Baptism of Christ* in the lunette. The tall campanile was originally a bastion of the Genoese fortifications.

A stepped walkway climbs to Monterosso's other notable monument, the Convento dei Cappuccini with its church of St Francis; inside are some works by lesser Ligurian masters, and a *Crucifixion* attributed to Van Dyck.

The Torre Aurora, on the hill of San Cristoforo, is all that remains of a wall circuit with 13 towers.

VERNAZZA

This is a charming port (*map B, C3*), interesting for its architecture—the cylindrical tower surmounting the Castel Doria on the point is one of Italy's oldest lighthouses (torches were burned at the top). It also has pleasant cafés on the harbour. The main street follows the covered Torrente Vernazzola and is crossed by a network of steep, sometimes stepped, lanes. Vernazza has always been the richest of the Cinque Terre and was for long the only safe haven. Established around 1000, it was a fief of the Obertenghi, then the Fieschi, before being taken, like Monterosso, by Genoa in the 13th century.

The most interesting place in town, architecturally, is the harbour square, flanked by colourful medieval houses, some with shady porticoes. The parish church of Santa Margherita d'Antiocha, on the landward side, was built on a rock overlooking the sea in the 11th century and renovated in the Gothic style in 1318. Its most distinctive trait is its 40m-tall campanile, based on the four pillars of the presbytery. The three-aisled interior has a Baroque altar, a wooden *Crucifix* attributed to Anton Maria Maragliano, and a 13th-century wooden *Immcolata*.

In the upper part of the town you can see some of the Genoese fortifications—traces of walls and two defensive towers.

STORMY WEATHER

Eleven victims, 26 municipalities affected, 730 million euro in damages, the streets of Monterosso and Vernazza filled with mud and debris to a height of 3–4m: this was the result of the flash floods that struck the Cinque Terre and other communities in southern Liguria and northern Tuscany on 25th October, 2011. At the climax of the storm the Riviera di Levante received 472mm of rain in six hours. The figure, recorded in Brugnato, represents a new Italian record (the previous record was 447mm, which fell at Genoa on October 8th, 1970). The rain gauge in Monterosso broke when it reached 315mm, so there are no official figures for the Cinque Terre, although unofficial sources report a total of c. 500mm.

The environmental group Legambiente firmly blamed the catastrophe on man, not nature. In Liguria over the last ten years, 46% of the farmland has been lost. The maintenance of stream beds has been overlooked and new building has occupied alluvial basins. It is not enough to blame farmers for giving up their land. All visitors, as 'users' of the Cinque Terre, are saddled with a broader responsibility. As tourism replaces farming as the primary source of income in this remarkable corner of the Italian coast the question looms large of who will maintain the area's 7000km of drystone walls, and who will tend the olives and vines on the terraces they support. If indeed this is a place of 'outstanding universal value', all of us are charged with finding the answer.

CORNIGLIA

Corniglia (*map B, C3*) was once an ancient Roman village. Perched on a striking bluff almost 200m high, it is the only one of the Cinque Terre without access from the sea. Pliny the Elder mentions its excellent wine in the *Naturalis Historia*, and archaeological excavations in Pompeii have turned up amphorae with the trademark 'Corenelia' stamped in the clay.

That Corniglia's economy has always been tied to the land rather than the sea is suggested by the fact that its narrow, cobbled lanes and humble houses have more in common with the villages of the mountainous interior than with the towns along the coast. In addition, to reach the village from the station you have to ascend a long brick staircase (377 stairs, forming 33 tree-shaded flights). The parish church of San Pietro, built in the 14th century over an 11th-century chapel, has a Baroque interior and sober Gothic exterior, with a fine rose window in white Carrara marble by the Tuscan stonecutters Matteo and Pietro da Campilio, who also made the carvings over the door. The picturesque main street ends at a scenic overlook with breathtaking views on three sides of the sea and coast.

South of Corniglia the Sentiero Azzurro follows the railway and the coast, entering the partly covered Sentiero dell'Amore, which began life as an explosives depot during the building of the railway. Walkers are better off climbing to the Alta Via (route no. 1) and its ramifications at Corniglia and descending at Riomaggiore, visiting Manarola by train when returning to their starting point.

MANAROLA

Manarola (*map B, C3*) enjoys a spectacular position with splendid views. Founded in the 12th century as a fief of the Genoese Fieschi family, the village is built on a rocky headland around the Torrente Volastra which, like the Buranco at Monterosso and the Vernazzola at Vernazza, flows beneath the main street. The little Sciacchetrà museum (*open March–Nov, daily 10–6*), halfway up the hill on the right, has interesting displays and a beautifully photographed video presentation of winemaking in the Cinque Terre. The steep little alleys are almost painfully picturesque, and there is a fine square at the top of the town, in front of the 14th-century Gothic church of the Natività di Maria Vergine (or San Lorenzo), offering fabulous views over the cascading rooftops to the sea.

RIOMAGGIORE

The most easterly of the Cinque Terre, Riomaggiore (*map B, C3*) seems to tumble down the cliffside into the water. Its layout is so precipitous that the fishermen have to pull their boats up into the streets in rough weather. The main street is squeezed tightly into the narrow valley of the (covered) Rio Major, and back lanes are so steep that most houses have two entrances—a front door at street level on the bottom floor, and a back door at street level on the top floor.

Tradition dates Riomaggiore's foundation to the 8th century; the first written documents describe its passage from the Fieschi to the Republic of Genoa in the 13th century. As a gateway to the Cinque Terre National Park, it has lost much of its traditional character as a fishing and farming town. The parish church of San Giovanni Battista dates from the 14th century; inside are some unexciting artworks of the 15th and 16th centuries, and a fine 19th-century Agati organ. The Italian landscape painter Telemaco Signorini, a member of the Tuscan Macchiaioli group, often stayed in this village, and Riomaggiore figures in several of his paintings.

IN THE HINTERLAND

Inland from the Cinque Terre, in the Val di Vara, are two very handsome villages that merit a visit for their culinary delights if for nothing else.

Brugnato (*map B, C2*) is 5mins from Autostrada A12 ('Brugnato–Borghetto Vara' exit) and is a good place to break your journey if you're travelling between Genoa and Rome or Florence. The seat of a bishop after 1133, it grew up in a circle around its cathedral and bishop's palace, and the street plan of the old fortified village is still visible. The diocese was moved to La Spezia in the 1920s but the former cathedral is still here: a two-aisled church built over two earlier churches, the oldest of which (the main aisle, now) is a 6th-century Byzantine construction. There are two frescoes and some carvings, and glass panels in the floor reveal the remains of the Benedictine monastery that was probably the first settlement here. The adjacent bishop's palace dates from the 12th century but was remodelled in the Baroque style in the 17th, the same century in which the monastery of San Francesco was founded. Come in June for the *Infiorata*, during the which floral compositions fill the streets.

Brugnato is known throughout Liguria for its pastries. *Cavagnetto*, or *cestinetto*, is the typical local Easter cake: it is a doughnut fitted with a handle, just like a small basket, with a boiled egg in the centre. The same dough is used to make *canestrello*, a cake flavoured with wild fennel.

Half an hour further up the Val di Vara is **Varese Ligure** (*map B, C2*), a pretty, colourful place built in a circle at the foot of its 15th-century castle of the Fieschi (well restored). This too was originally a fortified village, with houses arranged around a central square and presenting no doors or windows to the outside. The central square has long since been built over, but the atmosphere of the village remains that of a medieval *castrum*. A single-arched 16th-century bridge crosses the Torrente Crovana a few metres north of the castle, and at the Convento delle Monache Agostiniane the nuns make almond-based sweets, called *sciuette*, shaped like flowers. The recipe is a well-kept secret. Also unique to the village are *croxetti*, round pasta wafers impressed with floral designs and served in a walnut or pine-nut sauce.

THE GULF OF LA SPEZIA

One of the most beautiful places on the Riviera di Levante, the Gulf of La Spezia was once known as the Golfo di Venere; its modern nickname is the Golfo dei Poeti. This appellative was first coined, it seems, in 1910 by playwright Sem Benelli (*The Jester's Supper*), who spent his summers at San Terenzo. It recalls the fact that over the centuries many poets, writers and artists have been drawn to the gulf and the quiet little villages that speckle its shores. The list includes D.H. Lawrence, George Sand, Gabriele D'Annunzio, Byron, Shelley and J.M.W. Turner.

PORTOVENERE AND THE WEST SHORE

Portovenere (*map B, D3*), the ancient *Portus Veneris*, a dependency of Genoa since 1113, is a charming fortified village built on the sloping shore of the Bocchette, the narrow strait (114m wide) separating the Isle of Palmaria from the mainland. The houses overlooking the harbour, with their brightly coloured façades, are tall and narrow and there are no cross streets, just a few arcades with steep stairways connecting the single main street to the harbour of the beach, a reminder that this 'face' of the village was once also its main defence against attacks by sea.

On a rocky promontory at the southern end of the village, the restored 6th- and 13th-century church of **San Pietro** rises over the ruins of a temple of Venus. It commands a splendid view of Palmaria and the lofty cliffs of the Cinque Terre. The Grotto Arpaia, formerly beneath it, collapsed in 1932. It was known as 'Byron's Cave', for it was from here that the poet started his swim across the gulf to San Terenzo to visit Shelley at Casa Magni (*see below*) in 1822.

In the upper part of the village is the beautiful 12th-century church of **San Lorenzo**, above which (steep climb) towers the 16th-century **Castello Doria** (*open daily April–Nov 10.30–5.30*). It is now a cultural centre offering art exhibitions, conferences and performing arts events.

In the 14th century the Florentine painter Botticelli summered in **Fezzano**, near Portovenere, at the same time as Simonetta Vespucci (1453–76), the young Genoese noblewoman reputed to be the most beautiful lady of her time. The painter fell hopelessly in love with her—as did everyone who encountered her—and painted at least two portraits of her before her premature death, of consumption, at the age of 23. He is also thought to have used her as the model for his *Primavera* and the *Birth of Venus* (some say one can see the Gulf of La Spezia in the latter, with the promontories of Fezzano, Pezzino and Varignano on the goddess's left and the Isle of Palmaria on her right).

THE ISLAND OF PALMARIA

The rugged island of Palmaria can be visited by boat from Portovenere (boats are marked 'Traghetto Portovenere Isola Palmaria'; *www.barcaioliportovenere.com*). The island is noted for its gold-veined black *portoro* marble (the dark stone in the stripes of Genoese churches) and the traces of Mesolithic habitation found in the

Grotta della Colomba, one of its many caves. There are several walks to be taken amidst the fragrant *macchia mediterranea*, all offering absolutely stunning views of the sea and coast.

On a promontory at the north end of the island is the **Batteria fortificata Umberto I** (1887–9), one of the most important examples of 19th-century military architecture in southern Europe. Built in defence of the naval base at La Spezia, the battery was designed by military engineer Ferdinando Scapazzoni with the two sides exposed to fire completely embedded in the hillside, leaving only the hardened-iron turret showing. The battery was armed with two cannon capable of swivelling 270° and of firing 1000kg projectiles. The steam-driven service mechanisms necessary to rotate the turret and lift the heavy ammunition were powered by four boilers. The fortress, designed to accommodate a garrison of soldiers as well as the guns and their magazine, had a central hall for the storage and transportation of the ammunition, lateral rooms for machinery and equipment, and living and command space at the front. Restored after 2002 to plans by Laura Tamberi and Pier Giuseppe Galletto, the battery now holds a marine biology research laboratory run by the University of Pisa and a cultural centre open for exhibitions and events. The architecture is notable for the refined decorative scheme of the exterior (animal-headed gargoyles and rusticated stonework around doors and windows), and the barrel or dome vaulting of the interior, in brick or stone depending on the room's function.

Just off the island's south shore is the little **Isola del Tino**, with the remains of the 8th-century monastery of San Venerio. The island is owned by the navy and public access is only permitted on the feast day of the patron saint, on 13th Sept.

LERICI, TELLARO AND THE EAST SHORE

On the east shore of the gulf is the Bay of Lerici, with the fishing village of **San Terenzo** (*map B, D3*). There is a lovely seaside promenade here going all the way to (3km) Lerici. On a small cape is **Casa Magni**, the 'white house with arches' that was Shelley's last home, of which he was extremely fond. Mary Shelley wrote: 'I am convinced that the few months we passed there were the happiest he had ever known. He was never better than when I last saw him, full of spirits and joy, embark for Leghorn, that he might there welcome Leigh Hunt to Italy.' On that fateful voyage to Tuscany, on 8th July 1822, the 29-year-old Shelley and his friend Lieutenant Williams were drowned when their little schooner sank in a sudden squall. Their bodies were recovered on the beach near Viareggio, where they were cremated in the presence of Shelley's friends Trelawny, Byron and Leigh Hunt.

LERICI

Lerici (*map B, D3*) is a pleasant place with a spacious central piazza and a splendid 13th–16th century castle. Despite its popularity as a resort, its economy is still a mix of fishing, farming and tourism.

The name may come from *Erice*, son of Venus and Neptune, or by a different interpretation, from *Mons ilicis*, the ilex-clothed hill on whose slopes it is built. Certainly it was an important port in antiquity, and in the Middle Ages it was used by pilgrims joining the Via Francigena, the pilgrim route to Rome, at nearby Sarzana. It was a border post of the maritime Republic of Pisa until 1254, when the latter was defeated by the Republic of Genoa, and its strategic position made it a desirable possession for every political power active in the area in subsequent centuries. After being ceded by Pisa to Genoa it spent the 14th century under French rule, was sold to Florence and passed briefly through the hands of Alfonso V of Aragon before returning in 1479 to Genoa. It is at this time that the town was given its last circuit of walls and the castle was fortified with a thick curtain wall to make it invulnerable to artillery.

Today, of course, the border between Liguria and Tuscany is no longer a geopolitical hotspot and Lerici is simply a pretty seaside town with a complicated past. The castle is home to a **Museo Geopaleontologico** (*open Tues–Sun 10.30–1 & 4–7*), established after a twelve-year-old boy, on a hike, discovered some 220-milion-year-old dinosaur footprints in the hinterland here. In addition to some very beautiful fossils, the museum features spectacular dioramas of dinosaurs in their native environments and an earthquake simulation chamber illustrating the nature and effects of seismic events.

TELLARO

A coast road, running roughly parallel to a beautiful walking trail, goes on above the charming little bay of **Fiascherino** (where D.H. Lawrence lived in 1913–14) to **Tellaro** (*map B, D3*), a medieval village that rises sheer from the sea. Right on the rocks at the south end of the village, the pastel pink church of San Giorgio dates from the 16th century. A placque on the façade tells with telegraphic brevity a curious legend about the church. *Saraceni mare nostrum infestantes sunt noctu profligati quod polipus aer cirris suis sacrum pulsabat.* It seems Tellaro was saved from a night-time attack by Saracen pirates by a giant octopus that woke the population by ringing the church bells with its tentacles. The event is commemorated on the second Sun in August by the *Sagra del Polpo*, at which the hero of the story is eaten in various sauces but mainly *alla tellarese* (boiled and served with potatoes, olives, garlic, parsley, salt, pepper and lemon juice and the very fine local olive oil) or *all'inferno* (stewed with bay leaves, marjoram, pepper, tomatos and white wine). NB: Tellaro's population increases ten-fold in summer, from 800 to 8000, so plan your visit carefully.

WALKS FROM TELLARO

Several beautiful walks originate in Tellaro. Maps are available from the tourist information points in Lerici.

The **walk to La Serra** (*5km, elevation gain 150m; easy*) is mainly in the shade, making it good for warm summer days. From the central Piazza Matteotti, go east along the brick-paved Via Matteotti (Trail 3h), then climb the steep stony mule-path at the end of the village (this is the tough part) past a fine viewpoint overlooking the sea to the intersection with Trail 3. Turn left here and continue to climb, less steeply, over hill and vale, though olives and evergreen oaks to the the houses of Portesone, abandoned in the 16th century after an outbreak of plague. The trail on the left returns to Tellaro; continue under a collapsed fig tree and amidst olives and cypresses past the abandoned hamlet of Barbazzano (left; Trail 3r) and climb slightly through low forest to La Serra, again amidst olive groves. Here you can return to Tellaro via Barbazzano (though the trail may be overgrown in places) or to Lerici by bus.

The **walk to Montemarcello** (*5km, elevation gain 360m; moderately strenuous*) is all uphill, through *macchia mediterranea* and olive groves on the coast above Tellaro, then forests of oak and pine, further inland. Follow the walk to La Serra to the intersection with Trail 3, where you turn right. After a fairly level stretch, with good views of Tellaro and the sea, the trail curves left and climbs along a ridge, reaching the paved road at Zanego. Cross the road and continue uphill (on Trail 1), entering the forest beyond the Ristorante Pescarino. The trail continues on level ground at first, then climbs through the forest (keep an eye out for boar, particularly in the early morning when whole families browse for their breakfast). The trail turns abruptly right then follows a winding course to the little botanic garden at Monte Murlo, from which there is a fine view of the Alpi Apuane and the Versilia coast, in Tuscany.

Leaving the garden by the unpaved access road, turn immediately left on Trail 1, which leads via the cemetery to Montemarcello, a very pretty village of red and pink houses surrounded by olives (but once renowned for its delicious figs, in dialect *binèi*), with fine views of Tellaro and of the Gulf of La Spezia. No one knows quite when Montemarcello was founded; its regular street plan resembles that of Roman battle camp, and some say it is named in honour of the Roman Consul Marcus Claudius Marcellus, who killed the Gallic king Viridomarus at the battle of Clastidium (222 BC). The earliest written records of the village date from 1286, when a circuit of defensive walls was built; the walls of which you see vestiges today were built in 1485, under special permission from the Genoese senate. A marked path leads to Punta Corvo with a bird's-eye view of the coast; 700 wooden steps lead down to the grey-sand beach.

From the centre of Montemarcello steps descend to the head of Trail 3, twice crossing paved roads. Descend through the woods, returning shortly to the paved road; turn right and walk along the roadside for c. 100m before picking up the trail again and crossing the road once more as you climb to another good view point. Re-enter the woods on the trail and proceed more or less parallel to the paved road to Le Figarole; beyond, cross the road again to pick up your outbound trail, descending via Zanego to Tellaro.

AMEGLIA AND SARZANA

Ameglia (*map B, D3*), with its picturesque houses dominated by a 10th-century castle, overlooks the yacht basin at Bocca di Magra. In antiquity it was the port of **Luni**, a Roman town established on the site of a prehistoric settlement today famous for its statuary; its few, sunbaked ruins lie across the River Magra and the *autostrada* (*Via Luni 37, Ortonovo; open Tues–Sun 8.30–7.30*). Beyond the alluvial plain of the River Magra, in the hills, is the pretty old village of **Castelnuovo Magra** (*map B, D2*), whose church has a painting of the *Crucifixion* attributed to Van Dyck and a large *Calvary* by Brueghel the Younger. The old 13th-century Malaspina castle here has associations with Dante.

Sarzana (*map B, D2*) is an ancient fortified town, once of great strategic importance. It was the southeastern outpost of the Genoese Republic. The cittadella, a rectangular fort with six circular bastions, was rebuilt for the Florentine Lorenzo de' Medici in 1487 by Francesco di Giovanni; it is now a performing arts space known especially for its May music festival, *Musica e Suoni*. On the main Via Mazzini is the cathedral. It contains a panel painting of the *Crucifixion*, signed and dated 1138 by a certain Guglielmus, and 15th-century marble reliefs by Leonardo Riccomanni of Pietrasanta. Some of the paintings are by Domenico Fiasella, who was born here in 1589. Nearby is Sant'Andrea, the oldest monument in the town, probably dating from the 11th century. The 16th-century portal has pagan caryatids. The church of San Francesco, north of the town, contains the tomb by Giovanni di Balduccio of Guarnerio degli Antelminelli, son of Castruccio Castracani, who died as a child in 1322. Castracani was a great *condottiere*, who served a number of emperors in the Ghibelline cause. His romanticised and embellished biography was written by Machiavelli.

On a hill to the east is the massive **Fortezza di Sarzanello**, known as the Fortezza of Castruccio Castracani, restored by the Florentines in 1493 to designs by Francione and Luca del Caprina. It can be reached on foot from Via San Francesco by a pathway marked Montata di Sarzanello.

LA SPEZIA

La Spezia (*map B, D2–D3*), at the head of its fine gulf, has been one of the chief naval ports of Italy since a naval arsenal was built here in 1861. A provincial capital, the town—which was laid out in the late 19th century—forms a rectilinear L round a prominent hill. It is an interesting place for the study of early modern architecture, largely thanks to the work of one local master, Franco Oliva. Although born in Sardinia, this brilliant architect (and printmaker) lived most of his life in La Spezia, where he left a profound mark on the city's fabric. Co-editor of the Fururist magazine *L'Eroico* in 1911–13, he is one of the most original, and overlooked, architects of his time.

THE CATHEDRAL AND PALAZZO DEL GOVERNO
At the foot of the hill, by the sea, on Piazza Giovanni XXIII, is La Spezia's crown-like **Cattedrale di Cristo Re**, a contemporary design by Adalberto Libera. The Diocese of Luni, Sarzana and Brugnato was moved to La Spezia in 1929, but a satisfactory proposal for a new cathedral was produced only in 1956, by this prominent member of the Rationalist school. Libera died (at the age of 59) before ground was broken, and La Spezia found itself in the peculiar position of waiting, still, for its new cathedral to materialise nearly half a century after becoming the seat of a bishop. The present edifice was built in 1971–5 under the supervision of local architect Cesare Galeazzi, following Libera's 1956 design, which today looks rather dated. The circular plan is intended to symbolise the gathering of the faithful around Christ; the cylindrical

interior can accommodate 2,500 worshippers beneath its reinforced concrete roof, 50m in diameter and borne on twelve 8m cyclindrical piers, each of which bears the name of an Apostle. An 18th-century wooden *Crucifix* hangs above the high altar. Natural lighting is provided by the painted glass oculus in the ceiling and by a single ribbon window running round the perimeter walls. The local sculptor Lia Gisolini Godano designed the white marble high altar and ambo.

On the seaward side of the cathedral, overlooking Via Vittorio Veneto and the vast Piazza Europa, rises the **Palazzo del Governo**, designed in 1925 by Franco Oliva. The local government building, which owes a clear debt to the Viennese Secession style, was enriched in 1957 with stained-glass windows depicting scenes of local life in Roman, medieval and modern times, by Raffaela Albertella. Oliva's decorative programme includes the artificial stone façades (actually made of reinforced concrete), and the anthropomorphic statues and reliefs of eagles and angels, garlands and cyclopes that embellish them, all by the local sculptor Augusto Magli. Within, two parallel staircases lighted by bronze lamps lead up to the fist-floor halls where official business is conducted.

Overlooking the adjacent Piazza Verdi is Angiolo Mazzoni's **Palazzo delle Poste e dei Telegrafi** of 1933, a public building with a very different feeling. Mazzoni was Director of Works at the Ministry of Communications in Mussolini's Italy and designed a number of post offices and railway stations in the severe and imposing manner that typified Fascist public architecture. Some of his designs are quite successful; this one is heavy handed and confused. Fortunately, the interior holds a nice surprise: an extraordinary mosaic by the Futurists Luigi Fillia and Enrico Prampolini, around the monumental staircase. The mosaic, which seems to float on the brickwork, depicts communication and transportation by land, sea and air, in a splendid display of dynamic planes and lines, and warm colours.

TEATRO CIVICO AND THE CENTRO ARTE

A few blocks southwest, by the public gardens, is Franco Oliva's **Teatro Civico** of 1931–2. When first built it was used for phonograph and gramophone concerts as well as theatrical performances, and in 1953 it hosted the first colour movie shown in La Spezia. Oliva's design reinterprets the themes typical of 19th-century theatres (the portico and triangular tympanum outside, and the stalls, loggia and boxes inside) in a style that is at once austere and ironic, combining the elegant decoration of the now fading Viennese Secession style, with the clarity and precision of the new Rationalism. The domed ceiling can be rolled back on warm summer evenings.

Overlooking the adjacent Piazza Cesare Battisti is the **Centro Arte Moderna e Contemporanea** (*open Tues–Sat 10–1 & 3–7, Sun and holidays 11–7; camec.spezianet. it*). The permanent collection, on the second floor, is based on the Cozzani and Battolini bequests of modern and contemporary art, and the collection associated with the Golfo di La Spezia Prize, established by Filippo Tommaso Marinetti and Luigi Fillia in 1933. Here are represented early 20th-century Expressionist, Bauhaus and Surrealist artists, Italian classics such as Renato Guttuso, and most of the contemporary avant-garde movements such as Minimalism, Land Art, Arte Povera, Fluxus, European and Italian New Expressionism and Performance Art.

MUSEO NAVALE

The Naval Arsenal, the most important in Italy, was built by Domenico Chiodo in 1861–69. At the **Museo Tecnico Navale** here (*entrance next to the main gate; open daily 9–7.30*), models and relics collected since the Battle of Lepanto (1571) illustrate the marine history of Savoy and Italy. Among fascinating figureheads and other relics displayed on the ground floor is a magnificent set of ship models, including the caravelles *Niña, Pinta* and *Santa Maria* and a 1:50 scale model of the *Nave Scuola Amerigo Vespucci*, the Italian Navy's three-masted training ship, which is based in La Spezia. A highlight of the first-floor displays is the material from the ill-fated Arctic expedition of the *Airship Italia* piloted by Umberto Nobile: the dirigible was lost on 25th May 1928 over the North Pole; nine survivors of the crash were saved seven weeks later thanks to the ability to repair the radios (the airship had a separate transmitter and receiver), in a rescue effort whose extreme lack of coordination is now legend. Six more crew were trapped in the airship envelope, which drifted away after first impact, and have never been found. The polar explorer Roald Amundsen also vanished while flying to the crash zone to join the search. Here too are a fine collection of historic navigation instruments (compasses, sextants and octants). The more technical sections, on the ground floor and in the garden, are devoted to underwater warfare and naval artillery.

SANTA MARIA ASSUNTA AND THE TEATRO COZZANI

Santa Maria Assunta, the cathedral until 1975, was founded in 1271 but later rebuilt. All but destroyed in a 1943 bombing, the church, including its imposing grey-and-white striped west façade, was rebuilt to plans by Franco Oliva in a manner that makes maximum use of traditional materials and techniques. The church contains a large coloured terracotta altarpiece by Andrea della Robbia, whisked off to Arles in the Napoleonic period and returned to La Spezia in 1817 at the request of Vittorio Emanuele of Savoy.

Proceeding along the northwest leg of the 'L', you soon reach a theatre designed by Oliva a few years earlier, the 1919 **Teatro Cozzani** (*Piazza Cavour 45/46*). This wonderfully imaginative interpretation of the Secessionist style was specifically designed for the brothers Giulio and Virgilio Cozzani as a theatre and cinema. The main façade is adorned with reliefs by sculptors Augusto Magli and Angelo Del Santo and presents one of Oliva's little architectural *scherzi*: a bow window masking the projection room. Del Santo's frieze of dancing putti, on either side, deliberately quotes Donatello's *cantoria* for the cathedral of Florence, one of the great masterpieces of the Italian Renaissance. The foyer features an arch borne on marble arabesque columns, and the vaulted ceilings are decorated with paintings and friezes by local painter Luigi Agretti. The theatre was severely damaged in a 1943 bombing that destroyed the trussed roof and part of the ceiling paintings, and in recent years has been used as a bingo hall; it overlooks Gaspare Chiodo's immense **public market** (2005), in Piazza Cavour.

On nearby Via Sprugola (no. 10), stands Oliva's **Palazzo del Ghiaccio**, now a bank but originally built as an ice-making plant and cold-storage depot. The architect designed the building in 1920 in his signature austere-but-ironic style (notice the reliefs, by Augusto Magli, with dancing polar bears and marching penquins), which seems to warn that as important as architecture may be in the modern city, it should not be taken too seriously.

TWO MUSEUMS: AMEDEO LIA AND THE ARCHAEOLOGICAL MUSEUM

The **Museo Amedeo Lia** (*Via Prione 234, open Tues–Sun 10–6; museolia.spezianet. it*), opened in 1996 in the former monastery of the Minims of St Francis of Paola, contains an important collection (made since the 1940s) of antiquities, *objets d'art* and above all 13th–15th-century paintings, with an emphasis on gold-ground religious images and Italian primitives. The visit begins in the church, radically altered in the 19th century. Here are ivory and enamel pieces, jewellery, gold work, glasswork, small sculptures, miniatures from illuminated manuscripts. Upstairs a small room of Graeco-Roman antiquities leads into the painting collection, where highlights are a *St John the Baptist* by Bernardo Daddi (c. 1320); a lovely *Madonna and Child with Saints* by the Sienese painter Matteo di Giovanni (late 15th century); Sebastiano del Piombo's *Birth* and *Death of Adonis*, two panels probably made for a wedding chest (c. 1510); Tintoretto's *Lamentation over the Body of Christ*, so agitated it seems moved by gale-force winds (1556); Titian's *Portrait of a Man* (1510), whose wonderfully transparent veils of colour and skilful use of light create an extraordinary sense of psychological depth; a well-known self-portrait by Pontormo, painted on a terracotta tile (1520); a tiny oval *St Catherine of Alexandria* by Cranach the Elder, displayed in a suitably small room (c. 1530) and a curious architectural *capriccio* by Canaletto in which a vaguely northern European church rises through the mists of the Venetian lagoon. The second-floor rooms present glass and ceramic objects, and a *Wunderkammer*, or chamber of marvels.

On the spur of La Spezia's central hill, known simply as *Il Poggio* to locals, rises the Castello San Giorgio, a 14th-century fortification enlarged in the 15th and 16th centuries and restored as an exhibition space in the late 20th century. Here, on two floors, is the **Museo Archeologico** (*open summer, Mon 9.30–12.30, Wed–Sun, 10.30–1.30 & 5–8; winter Wed–Sun 9.30–12.30 & 2–5; museodelcastello.spezianet. it*). In the ground-floor rooms are interesting Ligurian statue-stelae of the Bronze and Iron Age, from a Lunigiana cult found on the River Magra, and Roman remains from Luni, from a seaside villa near Ameglia, and from other area sites. The upper floor displays the historic collections of Carlo and Carlo Andrea Fabbricotti, marble magnates from the Apuan Alps who financed many of the early excavations in southern Liguria and northern Tuscany. Here are abundant finds from Luni and its environs, ranging from architectural decorations to oil lamps and scent jars, busts and statues. There is also a fine collection of precious stones, and a large mosaic pavement, cut in the past into smaller pieces to adorn the floors of a private home.

PRACTICAL TIPS

WHERE TO STAY ON THE RIVIERA DI LEVANTE

CAMOGLI (*map B, B2*)

€€ Cenobio dei Dogi. An elegant establishment in a quiet part of town, with terraced park overlooking the sea. The hotel comes with three fine restaurants: Il Doge, La Playa and La Terrazza Giulia, the latter two open in summer only. All offer refined cuisine and beautiful views over the Golfo del Paradiso. *Via Cuneo 34, T: 0185 7241, www.cenobio.it.*

CHIESANUOVA/LEVANTO (*map B, C3*)

€€ La Sosta di Ottone III. This is a place for walkers, perched amidst olive-clad hills midway between Levanto and Monterosso, at the northern gateway to the Cinque Terre. The old village of Chiesanuova (1hr 30mins on foot or 10mins by taxi from Monterosso) is far enough from the tourist flow to be quiet and genuine, still marked by leisurely rhythms and old-fashioned lifestyles; the inn occupies a 16th-century listed building perfectly in step with its setting. There are just four rooms, each decorated in soft, soothing colours and each unique; and there is a tiny restaurant, where chef, sommelier and waiter are all the same person. *Località Chiesanuova 39, Levanto, T: 0187 814502, www.lasosta. com.*

€€ Stella Maris. Levanto, once a secluded bathing resort in a little bay, is now the busy northern gateway to the Cinque Terre. It has lovely gardens, and a good sandy beach, and preserves remains of its old walls along with a 13th–15th church. The Stella Maris is small and cosy, near the waterfront; its eight charming rooms have genuine antiques and, in some cases, painted ceilings. *Via Marconi 4, T: 0187 808258, hotelstellamaris.it.*

LERICI (*map B, D3*)

€€ Doria Park. This modern establishment is set in an olive grove just above the town centre; quiet and restful, it overlooks the rooftops and the Golfo dei Poeti. The rooms on the front have sea views; those on the back open on the lush green park. *Via Doria 2, T: 0187 967 124, www.doriahotels. com.*

MANAROLA (*map B, C3*)

€ La Torretta. Small, intimate and romantic, at the very top of the town with stunning views over sea, houses and vineyards. The name refers to the building, a 17th-century tower house, furnished in a tasteful mix of antique and contemporary styles. At the moment this is far and away the best place to stay in the Cinque Terre. Closed Jan and Feb. *Piazza della Chiesa, Vico Volto 20, T: 0187 920327, www.torrettas.com.*

PORTOFINO (*map B, B2*)

€€€€ Splendido & Splendido Mare. Taken together, these two siblings form one of the top European luxury hotels. The Splendido, established in 1901 in a former private villa, is surrounded by gardens above the town, with magnificent views in all directions; the Splendido Mare, down by the harbour, offers a more informal atmosphere. The Splendido is traditionally the hotel of the stars: some say it has seen more celebrity love stories than any other piece of real estate on the planet. A meal at the restaurant, La Terrazza, may cost you more than your airfare to Italy, but the garden is more than *splendido* and the view is unforgettable. *Salita Baratta 16, T: 0185 267801, www. hotelsplendido.com.*

€€ **Eight.** The nice thing about staying in Portofino is that the crowds evaporate at dusk leaving you to enjoy a solitary evening stroll by the harbour, or up to the little church of San Giorgio. This small hotel is the perfect setting for the experience: a beautifully renovated townhouse by the water, with simple but elegant rooms decorated in the warm pastels of Portofino. *Via del Fondaco 11, T: 0185 26991, portofino.eighthotels.it.*

PORTOVENERE (*map B, D3*)
€€ **Belvedere.** Have you ever wondered what the youngest captain in the Italian Navy did when he retired? The answer is this: a warm, family-run place with sea views and good restaurant. Everything here is simple, straightforward and genuine. The food is delicious. *Via Garibaldi 26, T: 0187 790608, www.belvedereportovenere.it.*

RAPALLO (*map B, B2*)
€€€ **Excelsior Palace Hotel.** Built in 1902 as the Kursaal Rapallo, this was Italy's first casino; the façades, ornamentation and halls of the Art Nouveau building are characteristic of the taste of its time. In 1917 it hosted the Rapallo Convention leading to the creation of the Supreme War Council, the central command created by the British Prime Minister David Lloyd George to coordinate Allied military strategy during the First World War. Other guests have included Hemingway, Marconi, the Duke of Windsor with Wallis Simpson, King Hussein of Jordan, Constantine of Greece, and Rita Hayworth. Thornton Wilder worked on *The Matchmaker* here. *Via San Michele di Pagana 8, T: 0185 230666, www.excelsiorpalace.it.*

€€ **Hotel Riviera.** A smaller Art Nouveau creation, the 1905 Riviera occupies a corner lot overlooking the seaside promenade. Behind its wrought-iron balconies, mansard roofs and carved window frames are just 20 rooms. Ernest Hemingway wrote 'Cat in the Rain', one of his *First Forty-Nine Stories,* here in 1923. Ezra Pound, King Juan Carlos of Spain, Elettra Marconi and the environmentalist-adventurer Sir Peter Blake, who was killed by pirates while monitoring environment change on the Amazon in 2001, all stayed here. The restaurant, Il Gambero, is rightly famous. *Piazza IV Novembre 2, T: 0185 50248, www. hotelrivierarapallo.com.*

SANTA MARGHERITA LIGURE (*map B, B2*)
€€€ **Hotel Imperiale Palace.** The Belle Époque façades of this grand old place have marked the skyline of Santa Margherita since 1889. Luigi Pirandello and Eleonora Duse, Simone Signoret and Ives Montand, and Humphrey Bogart and Lauren Bacall all made this their home on the riviera. The Novecento restaurant is rightly reputed superb, and the Art-Nouveau furnishings of the Caffè del Trattato are worth the steep prices of a coffee or an *aperitivo* here. *Via Pagana 19, T: 0185 288991, www.hotelimperiale.com.*

€€ **Grand Hotel Miramare.** Built in 1903 in a transitional style between Beaux-Arts and Art Nouveau, this big white establishment has painted *trompe l'oeil* and floral decorations on its façades and in its exquisitely furnished halls and restaurant, and lush gardens overlooking the sea. Marconi made the world's first telegraph and radio-telephone transmissions from the terrace (1933). *Lungomare Milite Ignoto 30, T: 0185 287013, www.grandhotelmiramare.it.*

€€ Jolanda. Not in the best location (in the historic city centre, so lacking views of the sea and greenery), but warm and friendly with a good restaurant. *Via Costa 6, T: 0185 287513, www.hoteljolanda.it.*

SESTRI LEVANTE (*map B, B2*)

€€ Grand Hotel Villa Balbi. The 17th-century villa of one of the most eminent Genoese patrician families, this fine old hotel overlooks Sestri's lovely waterfront. Many of the original interior decorations (including frescoes ceilings in some of the rooms) have been preserved. Absolutely sumptuous breakfasts are served in the large, luxuriant park. *Viale Rimembranza 1, T: 0185 42941, www.villabalbi.it.*

€€ Grand Hotel dei Castelli. This Gothic-revival castle in its shady park was created in the 1920s by financier Riccardo Gualino, a friend and supporter of Guglielmo Marconi. At Gualino's invitation Marconi set up a laboratory in a tower here, and in 1934 conducted the first successful experiment in radio navigation, guiding the steamship *Electra* between two buoys, 100m apart, in the sea off the point. Rooms are handsomely furnished, the park is gorgeous, the restaurant is excellent (with good views), there is a salt-water pool, but sea bathing is strictly on the rocks. *Via*

alla Penisola 26, T: 0185 485780, www.hoteldeicastelli.it.

€€ Miramare. Right on the beach of the peaceful Baia del Silenzio, this former patrician mansion is calm and comfortable. The restaurant is excellent and offers summer seating on a lovely terrace overlooking the water. *Via Cappellini 9, T: 0185 480855, www.miramaresestrilevante.com.*

€€ Vis à Vis. In an elevated position on a headland amid olive groves, this elegant family-run establishment offers good views over the town and sea, and two fine restaurants: the Olimpo in-house and the Portobello by the private beach. *Via della Chiusa 28, T: 0185 42661, www.hotelvisavis.it.*

TELLARO (*map B, D3*)

€€ Il Nido. Surrounded by olive and pine groves 4km outside town, this little contemporary hotel enjoys breathtaking views of the coast and water. The rooms are bright and cheerful and it has its own secluded little beach. There's no in-house restaurant, but the beachfront bar offers a wide variety of large salads and foccaccia-based sandwiches, and Tellaro is 10mins away on foot. *Via Fiascherino 75, Località Fiascherino, T: 0187 969263, www.hotelnido.com.*

VERNAZZA (*map B, C3*)

€€ La Malà. Vernazza is considered the prettiest of the Cinque Terre and it's the only one with a real harbour, tiny though it is. La Malà is the finest accommodation in town: located in the neighbourhood of Luvegu, at the opposite end of the village, it's a five-minute walk from the hustle and bustle of the harbour. The ancient house has been beautifully renovated to make four bedrooms and a rustic stone terrace overlooking the village and the sea. *Via San Giovanni Battista 29, T: 334 287 5718, www.lamala.it.*

Comfortable apartments to rent in Santa Margherita and Portofino can be found on www.homelidays.it.

WHERE TO EAT ON THE RIVIERA DI LEVANTE

NB: Many hotels also have restaurants. Many are described in the section above.

CAMOGLI (*map B, B2*)
For the Cenobio dei Dogi, see above. Otherwise there are plenty of restaurants, bars and pizza places on the waterfront.

CHIAVARI (*map B, B2*)
€€ **Gran Caffè Defilla.** Defilla is the largest café in town and possibly in all of Liguria: its elegant Art-Nouveau premises, with their stuccoes, mirrors and straight-backed wood Chiavarine chairs (a form invented in 1807 by local artisan Giuseppe Gaetano Descalzi) occupy an entire city block of the arcaded corso. Once frequented by film stars (Rita Hayworth) and political heavyweights (Italian presidents Antonio Segni and Sandro Pertini), it is still a feature of upper-crust social life in the Ligurian Levant. *Corso Garibaldi 4, T: 0185 309829, www. grancaffedefilla.it.*

€ **Antica Osteria Luchin.** This simple *osteria*, with its tables laid beneath the arcades, was established a century ago by a baker's boy, Luchin Bonino, and has been legendary ever since for its *farinata*, a wood-oven-baked cake of chickpea flour, water, olive oil and salt—although the menu has diversified over the years to include other comfort foods, such as *polpetone* (meatloaf) and minestrone. It has long been a magnet for artists and writers (notoriously hungry and broke), and the classic Italian cinema crowd—Michelangelo Antonioni, Vittorio Gassman, Mario

Soldati and their friends—made it their hideout during the 1950s and 1960s. *Via Bighetti 51, T: 0185 301063, www. luchin.it.*

LA SPEZIA (*map B, D2–D3*)
€€ **La Posta.** An elegant restaurant serving refined dishes, in the heart of the historic city centre just a few paces away from Piazza Verdi. The menu tends to favour fish, and there are two chefs, both Japanese. *Via Don Minzoni 24, T: 0187 760437, www. lapostadiclaudio.com.*

LERICI (*map B, D3*)
€€ **Conchiglia.** An outstanding traditional seafood restaurant, with warm atmosphere, good service and outside seating in fair weather. *Piazza del Molo 3, T: 0187 967334, www. laconchiglialerici.it.*

€€ **Dei Pescatori.** The best place to go, on this coast, on a summer evening. The owners really are fisherfolk (with their own boat) and the all-you-can-eat dinners, served swiftly and cordially *al fresco*, on the town's main square, are remarkable for their quality as well as quantity. An after-dinner stroll along the waterfront is recommended; a long drive is not, as the house wine is also quite good. *Via Doria 6, T: 0187 965534.*

€€ **Frantoio.** This restaurant in an old olive press combines delicious regional cooking with warm, friendly service and quiet, understated décor. Located on a narrow lane around the corner from the main square, it's centrally located but easy to miss. *Via Cavour 21, T: 0187 964174, www. ristoranteilfrantoiolerici.it.*

PORTOFINO (*map B, B2*)

€€€ Caffè Ristorante Bar Excelsior. This 'American bar' on the piazzetta was established in 1924 to serve Portofino's earliest élite visitors, the scions of the Colonna, Borghese and Torlonia families remembered for their patronage of Renaissance and Baroque artists. For them, proprietor Lina Repetta invented a new summer delight made from vanilla and raspberry-cream ice-cream, fresh raspberries and grenadine syrup; asked what she called it, she replied in Genoese dialect, '*u lé un paciugo*' (oh, it's a fine mess). And so was born *paciugo* ice-cream. After the war, right up till the 1970s, the Hollywood set made this their home-away-from-home. *Piazza Martiri dell'Olivetta 54, T: 0185 269005, www.caffexcelsior.it.*

€€€ Ristorante Lo Stella. The competition. Slightly less chic, slightly more aristocratic (customers: Princess Soraya, the Duke and Duchess of Windsor, King Juan Carlos), easy to reach from your yacht without going into the village. This century-old establishment, in the same family for eight generations, draws gourmets as well as the rich and famous, thanks to its exquisite traditional seafood dishes. *Molo Umberto I 3, T: 0185 269007, www.lostellaristorante.com.*

€€ Da Puny. Not cheap, but not as expensive you might fear, considering the venue: one of Italy's finest traditional seafood restaurants, with superb views of the country's most picturesque town and its little bay. *Piazza Martiri dell'Olivetta 5–7, T: 0185 269037.*

€€ Taverna del Marinaio. This place can be as stylish or as informal as you like: both styles are comfortably accommodated. Good Ligurian pesto, salads, seafood and desserts. Right by the waterfront, under the arcade. *Piazza Martiri dell'Olivetta 36. T: 0185 269103, www.tavernadelmarinaio.com.*

PORTOVENERE (*map B, D3*)

See **€€ Belvedere**, above.

RAPALLO (*map B, B2*)

€€ Da Monique. A down-to-earth, traditional restaurant with good seafood and nice views. You won't be alone on weekend evenings, so be sure to reserve. *Lungomare Vittorio Veneto 6, T: 0185 50541, www. ristorantemonique.it.*

€ Enoteca Il Castello. An excellent wine bar right on the water, with smashing views of its namesake and lots of good things to nibble on. Good for an *aperativo*, a light meal, or a late-night snack. *Lungomare Castello 6, 0185 52426.*

RECCO (*map B, B2*)

€€ Manuelina. A tavern established here in 1885 quickly acquired a reputation amongst the sea-captains of the Riviera di Levante. Before long vacationing industrialists discovered it, and in the 1960s and 1970s it was a favourite dining place for actors. By this time its delicious cheese focaccia had won a number of culinary prizes. Now run by the fourth generation of the founding family, it hosts a prize of its own, the Premio Giovanni Rebora for gastronomy, which includes sections for those who study and write about food. *Via Roma 278, T: 0185 74128/75364, www.manuelina.it.*

€€ Da Ö Vittorio. This bastion of Ligurian tradition has stood in the same place since 1895, despite the 27 bombing raids that devastated Recco in the Second World War. The *focaccia di Recco* is legendary, but everything on the menu is delicious, prepared with the freshest ingredients and in full respect of the historic recipes of the *terroir*. Equally historic is the clientèle, which includes politicians, sportsmen and musicians, many of whom are portrayed on the walls. *Via Roma 160, T: 0185 74029/75896, www.daovittorio. it.*

SARZANA (*map B, D2*)

€€ La Compagnia dei Balenieri. This is more than just a good *trattoria* specialising in regional recipes; everything here is cool, from the décor (faux-marble walls hung with ship paintings) to the table settings (traditional crockery on striped tablecloths) to the ironic/ iconic trademark (the image of the 'company' standing on a whale). Preparation, presentation and service are impeccable. *Via Rossi 28, T: 0187 603537.*

€ Pasticceria Gemmi il Loggiato. Established in 1840 by Swiss confectioners in a historic palace in the old town, this is an unusual place: *pasticceria* on the ground floor, restaurant on the floor above. Here you'll find all the classic creations from Sarzana's historic art of patisserie, including *spungata di Sarzana* (a soft Christmas cake filled with dried fruit and fruit preserves, almonds and pine-nuts, and believed to be based on a Roman recipe) and *buccellato di Sarzana* (a simple ring-shaped cake taking its name from the Latin *bucellatum*, soldier's bread). The loggiato offers open-air seating for the restaurant in summer and is a venue for events connected with Sarzana's

literary and music festivals, including the international competition for young opera singers. *Via Mazzini 21, T: 0187 620165.*

SANTA MARGHERITA LIGURE (*map B, B2*)

€€ Da Gennaro. Popular, lively pizzeria which also serves good pasta dishes, meat and fish, and local, fresh produce in season. *Piazza Martiri della Libertà 30, T: 0185 286951.*

€€ Oca Bianca. A restaurant for meat and pasta lovers. Good homemade food. Look out for the ceramic white geese. Evenings only. Closed Mon. *Via XXV Aprile 21, T: 0185 288411, www. ristoranteocabianca.net.*

€ Caffè del Porto. In business since 1945 on the main waterfront, serving local fishermen as well as visitors. A lovely old-fashioned place, perfect for a glass of wine and a plate of nibbles, or a simple meal. *Via Bottaro 32.*

€€ L'Insolita Zuppa. Home-made ravioli, freshly-caught fish and grilled meat. They are also proud of their crema catalana. Cheerful and well-liked. Closed Wed. *Via Romana 7, T: 0185 289594, www.insolitazuppa.it.*

€ Pestarino. A fine place for coffee and cakes. Sit inside in winter, outside in the piazza opposite the church of Nostra Signora della Rosa in summer. *Via Palestro.*

SESTRI LEVANTE (*map B, B2*)

€€ El Pescador. ▪ The walk out to this restaurant in a low white building at the foot of the rock by Sestri's harbour is almost as wonderful as the meal that awaits you. The ambience is yacht-clubbish, with the odd capstan and compass, but the food is genuine, and genuinely delicious: scallops, prawns and freshly-caught fish accompanied by pine nut *battuto* and Taggia olives.

Wines are mainly Italian, many of them Ligurian, from the Riviera di Ponente. *Via Queirolo 1, T: 0185 42888, www. ristoranteelpescador.com.*

€ **Rossignotti.** This fine pastry shop and confectioner offers its clients two locations in the historic town centre: an older one (1840) on Via XXV Aprile, and a newer one (1900) at the corner of Via XXV Aprile and Viale Dante. The latter comes complete with varnished pitch-pine furniture, Art Nouveau Baccarat vases, and statues of the *Four Seasons* in the shop window. Everything here is delicious, but the family-run firm is particularly well-known for its hard candies, chocolates and nougat. *www.rossignotti1840.it.*

VERNAZZA (*map B, C3*)

€€ **Gianni Franzi** (with rooms). The number of hikers per square meter of flat ground in the Cinque Terre is beyond belief, and the impact of the throngs on the quality of services is noticeable. In this context Gianni Franzi is swimming against the current, holding on steadfastly to the high standards of quality for which he has been known for years. Expect creative interpretations of traditional Ligurian recipes—and a long wait if you haven't reserved. *Piazza Marconi 5, T: 0187 812228, www.giannifranzi.it.*

Practical Information

ARRIVAL AND GETTING AROUND

WHEN TO GO

The best time to visit Liguria is out of season: late February can be glorious (though many hotels are still closed). Spring is superb. All the resorts get crowded at Easter time and summer is very hot and crowded. Late autumn and winter are typically wet, windy and cold.

TRANSPORT

By air: Genoa is at the geographic centre of Liguria, and this makes its airport (*www. airport.genova.it*), at Sestri Ponente 6km west of the city, particularly convenient. Buses (Volabus) run every half hour between the airport and Piazza Principe station (*for details, see www.genovaairport.com*). Nice airport can be a good choice if you're headed for the Riviera di Ponente; Volpibus has services two or three times daily in summer to San Remo, Imperia, Albenga, Savona and Genoa. If your destination is the Riviera di Levante, consider flying to Pisa (*www.pisa-airport.com*). The airport is only 8mins by shuttle bus from Pisa Central Station, from which trains run to the Cinque Terre in c. 1hr and to Santa Margherita Ligure/Portofino in c. 2hrs.

By car: Liguria can be reached by the A10 (Autostrada dei Fiori) from France, A6 from Turin, A26 from Alessandria; A7 from Milan and A12 from Pisa. All these highways, given the nature of the terrain, have plenty of curves, viaducts and tunnels. Commercial traffic can be heavy on weekdays, and major (10–40km) tailbacks of sun-seekers from Milan and Turin are common on Sat mornings and Sun afternoons in June–Sept. If you plan to spend most of your time visiting the coastal resorts, you will not need a car. The railway runs close to the coast and services are frequent (*see below*).

By rail: The main line from Rome to Paris follows the Tyrrhenian coast to Genoa, then continues via Turin to Paris. Fast Eurostar trains cover the 500km from Rome to Genoa in c. 4hrs. Genoa is also on the main line to Italy from southern France; from Nice to Genoa takes c. 3hrs. The French TGV runs as far as Menton, making it possible to reach Genoa from Paris in 9–10hrs. Genoa enjoys frequent connections also to Milan and Turin, both of which can be reached in 1hr 40mins.

Trains within Liguria itself are quick, frequent and good value. All the main resorts have railway stations, many of them very close to—or right within—the town centres. The Cinque Terre is also accessible by rail. Intercity trains link Ventimiglia at one end of Liguria with La Spezia at the other in under 4hrs, with many intermediate stops. For information, prices and timetables, see the Italian railway website (*www.trenitalia.com*).

Paper (i.e. not electronic) tickets which do not show a date and time (in other words, open-validity tickets) must be validated at the stamping machines on the station platform before you board. The aim of this is to prevent you using the ticket again or to enable you to claim a refund in case the train fails to depart. You can be fined if you forget to validate.

By bus: Some parts of Liguria where the trains don't go are served by bus. Buses can be useful, for example, for getting between Rapallo, Santa Margherita and Portofino. Buses link Portofino and Santa Margherita in 15–20mins, with a handful of services continuing to Rapallo (otherwise change at Santa Margherita). The same company, ATP, has services linking Sestri Levante with Varese Ligure in about an hour. For routes and timetables, see *www.atpesercizio.it*.

By sea: Information about boats and ferries between the various Ligurian ports are given in the relevant chapters of this guide. There are various companies that offer boat trips around the Cinque Terre, Portofino peninsula and Portovenere. For details, fares and timetables, visit the websites: *www.navigazionegolfodeipoeti.it* (for Portovenere, Portofino and the Cinque Terre); *www.golfoparadiso.it* (for Genoa, the Portofino peninsula and Cinque Terre); *www.liguriaviamare.it* and *www.whalewatchliguria.it/turismo* (for a variety of excursions including whale watching).

DISABLED TRAVELLERS

All new public buildings in Italy are obliged to provide facilities for the disabled. Historic buildings are more difficult to convert, and access difficulties still exist. Hotels that cater for the disabled are indicated in tourist board lists. Airports and railway stations provide assistance, and certain trains are equipped to transport wheelchairs. Access to town centres is allowed for cars with disabled drivers or passengers, and special parking places are reserved for them.

LOCAL INFORMATION

Italy is undergoing an administrative reform that will do away with the province as an intermediate unit of government. No one yet seems to know what will happen to the provincial tourist boards, the traditional hubs of tourist information. At the time of writing the main sites (with links to local tourist boards) are:

All destinations: Turismo Liguria, www.turismoinliguria.it

Genoa: Visit Genoa, www.visitgenoa.it

Imperia and environs: Riviera dei Fiori, www.visitrivieradeifiori.it

Savona and environs: Riviera delle Palme, turismo.provincia.savona.it
Riviera di Levante: www.turismoprovincia.laspezia.it
Cinque Terre: www.cinqueterre.it.

VISITOR CARDS

The **Genoa Museum Card** gives free or reduced admission to selected museums and cultural venues. There are 24hr and 48hr versions, with or without public transport included. Museum cards are on sale at participating museums, the bookshop of the Musei di Strada Nuova, main railway stations in Liguria, and main AMT ticket offices, or online at Visit Genoa: www.visitgenoa.it/en/store.

The **Cinque Terre Trekking Card** affords unlimited access to the park trail system, guided tours, bus service within villages, pay toilets, workshops at the Park Centre for Environmental Education and WiFi (at park hotspots) as well as reduced admission to the civic museums of La Spezia. The Cinque Terre Carta Treno MS offers the same benefits plus unlimited access to Regionali and Regionali Veloci trains between Levanto and La Spezia (in second class only). The cards come in one- and two-day versions and there are discounts for young people and seniors (*for details, see www.cinqueterre.eu.com*).

ACCOMMODATION

A short selection of hotels, chosen on the basis of character or location, is given at the end of each chapter. They are classified as follows: €€€€ (€900 or over), €€€ (€350–900), €€ (€150–300) or € (€150 or under). It is advisable to book well in advance, especially between May and October; if you cancel the booking with at least 72 hours' notice you can claim back part or all of your deposit. Service charges are included in the rates. By law breakfast is an optional extra, although a lot of hotels will include it in the room price. When booking, always specify if you want breakfast or not.

BLUE GUIDES RECOMMENDED

Hotels, restaurants and *osterie* that are particularly good choices in their category—in terms of excellence, location, charm, value for money or the quality of the experience they provide—carry the Blue Guides Recommended sign: ▪. All these establishments have been visited and selected by our authors, editors or contributors as places they have particularly enjoyed and would be happy to recommend to others. To keep our entries up-to-date, reader feedback is essential: please do not hesitate to contact us (*www. blueguides.com*) with any views, corrections or suggestions, or join our online discussion forum.

FOOD & DRINK

Italian food is usually good and inexpensive. Generally speaking, the least pretentious *ristorante* (restaurant), *trattoria* (small restaurant) or *osteria* (inn or tavern) provides the best value. A selection of restaurants is given at the end of each chapter. Prices are categorised as follows: €€€€ (€80 or more per head), €€€ (€60–80), €€ (€40–50) and € (€30 or under).

Prices on the menu do not include a cover charge (shown separately, usually at the bottom of the page), which is added to the bill. The service charge (*servizio*) is now almost always automatically added at the end of the bill; tipping is therefore not strictly necessary, but a few euro are appreciated. Note that many simpler establishments do not offer a written menu.

RESTAURANTS IN LIGURIA:
FROM FARINATA STALLS TO MICHELIN STARS

Food is very good in Liguria (*see Regional Cuisine, below*) and there are establishments to suit all palates and pockets, from humble *farinata* stalls and bakeries selling foccaccia and *torta salata*, through taverns where you can get a hearty plate of pasta with pesto, to fine restaurants boasting Michelin stars. At the time of writing the Michelin-starred restaurants on the two rivieras were as follows:

On the Riviera di Ponente
Paolo e Barbara in San Remo (*www.paolobarbara.it*);
La Conchiglia in Arma di Taggia (*www.laconchigliaristorante.eu*);
Agrodolce in Oneglia (*Calata Cuneo 25, T: 0183 293702*);
San Giorgio in Cervo (*Via Alessandro Volta 19, T: 0183 400175*);
Il Palma in Alassio (*www.ilpalma.com*);
Il Vescovado in Noli (*www.hotelvescovado.it/ristorante.php*);
Claudio in Bergeggi (*xoomer.virgilio.it/htlclaudio/ristorante.html*);
21.9 in Albissola Marina (*www.ristorante21punto9.it*);
The Cook in Arenzano (*www.thecook.it*).

On the Riviera di Levante
Mauro Ricciardi alla Locanda dell'Angelo in Ameglia (*www.chefmauroricciardi.com*).

Nevertheless, if you're looking for a good, simple meal, not everywhere is as authentic as it might be. There has been a lot of soul-searching lately over the low quality of food and accommodation in Ligurian resorts, many of which have remained tied to the 1960s' mass-tourism business model. Camogli, Tellaro, Lerici and Santa Margherita generally have a high-quality offering, but the Cinque Terre are notoriously overpriced and the quality of supply is disappointingly low. The same can be said for San Remo and the other famous resorts on the Riviera di

Ponente. It is not always as easy here as it is in other regions of Italy to make specific recommendations.

BARS AND CAFÉS

Bars and cafés are open from early morning to late at night and serve a variety of drinks and snacks that are usually taken standing at the bar. In traditional establishments you pay the cashier first, then present your receipt to the barman in order to get served; but in practice, in many places, the barman and cashier are one and the same. It is customary to leave a small tip on the counter. If you sit at a table the charge is usually higher, and you will be given waiter service (so don't pay first). However, some simple bars have a few tables that can be used with no extra charge, and it is always best to ask, before ordering, whether there is waiter service or not.

COFFEE

Italy has some of the best coffee in Europe. *Caffè* or *espresso* (black coffee) can be ordered *alto* or *lungo* (diluted), *corretto* (with a liquor), or *macchiato* (with a dash of hot milk). A *cappuccino* is an *espresso* with more hot milk than a *caffè macchiato* and is generally considered a morning drink. A glass of hot milk with a dash of coffee in it, called *latte macchiato* is another early-morning favourite. In summer, many drink *caffè freddo* (iced coffee).

REGIONAL CUISINE

Tuscans and Ligurians can come to blows when talking about olive oil. What the former consider the distinctive features of freshly pressed oil—its spicy tang and rich flavour—the latter consider rather crass and vulgar, arguing that the lighter, more delicately flavoured Ligurian oil can do anything Tuscan oil can do, as well as enhance the subtler flavours of fresh fish and vegetables. Foreigners—which term includes Italians from non-oil-producing regions such as Piedmont and Lombardy—must let the issue of which oil is *better* blow on the Mediterranean breeze. The fact is, the two are noticeably *different* (and the unobtrusive Ligurian oil does go very well with fish).

Ligurian cooking is *povera*, 'poor', in terms of ingredients, but rich in imagination. The best regional dishes are prepared with local olive oil and seasoned with fresh spices, many of which grow wild in the rocky, sun-baked hills. Partly because of the region's history of material poverty, and partly because imagination rarely respects traditional boundaries, little distinction is made in Liguria between appetisers, first courses and main courses. In fact the region's two great contributions to Italian cuisine are *focaccia*, the low, soft, salty bread that can be used as a support for just about anything (the cheese-filled *focaccia di Recco* is so special its making is overseen and protected by a *Comitato di Autenticità*), and *torta salata*, the 'savoury pie' that can be filled with anything and everything but is particularly good when stuffed with fresh spring greens. Here in Liguria, when you go to a bar for an aperitif, you will often be brought so many delicious nibbles to go with it that dinner recedes ever further into the night.

Also distinctive of this region is *pesto*, the famous sauce made from fresh basil, garlic, pine nuts and ewe's cheese and served with *trofie, trenette* or other pastas. It is completely different from the pesto that comes in a jar, being softer, creamier and a much paler green in colour. Go to a Ligurian greengrocer or even a supermarket for basil, and you will find huge fresh bouquets of it on offer, the stems wrapped in dampened paper to keep it crisp.

A signature Ligurian dish is *cappon magro* (a monumental creation built in layers, with ingredients from the land—various vegetables, pine nuts, capers, olives, parsley, oil and vinegar—and from the sea—sliced boiled fish and sometimes shellfish—assembled over a sailer's hardtack biscuit to form a dome or pyramid). Other good things to try in Liguria are *corzetti* or *corxetti* (a small round, flat pasta usually dressed with butter, sweet marjoram and pine nuts, but also with the rich, spicy meat sauce *töcco*); *buridda di seppie* (sliced cuttlefish cooked with olive oil, tomatoes, spices and fresh peas); *coniglio in umido* (rabbit browned in olive oil and butter, then stewed with garlic, rosemary, onion, white wine, black olives and pine nuts); *vitello all'uccelleto* (diced veal browned in olive oil and butter, with bay, white wine and sliced artichokes, when in season); *pandolce* (Ligurian panettone, less fluffy than the Milanese cake, with plenty of candied fruit and raisins) and *latte alla crema* (a rich vanilla and cinnamon custard, served in a deep bowl).

WINE

Ligurian wines also stand apart from the crowd. The lie of the land in Liguria—this strip of steep hills hinged between sea and mountains—makes all farming, and especially grape-growing, difficult. Ligurian wines are therefore made in small quantities, and can be quite expensive. The growing districts are located at the two ends of the region: the Riviera di Levante produces the Colli di Luni white and red; the Colline di Levanto and Golfo del Tigullio red, white and rosé; as well as the legendary Cinque Terre DOC whites (made from Vermentino, Bosco and Albarola grapes). The strong, sweet Sciacchetrà, made from dried grapes, is particularly distinctive, but it is produced in such limited quantities that an authentic bottle can cost an arm and a leg (beware of imitations). The Riviera di Ponente makes Vermentino, Pigato, Ormeasco and Rossese di Dolceacqua. This is undoubtedly the finest Ligurian wine. It takes its name from a small village in the Valle Nervina but is made throughout Imperia province and around Ventimiglia. It is a light, sincere red, with a colour somewhere between ruby and garnet and a soft, aromatic, warm flavour. It is made in very small quantities.

ADDITIONAL INFORMATION

PUBLIC HOLIDAYS

Italian national holidays are as follows:

    1 January
    Easter Sunday and Easter Monday
    25 April (Liberation Day)

1 May (Labour Day)
2 June (Festa della Repubblica)
15 August (Assumption)
1 November (All Saints' Day)
8 December (Immaculate Conception)
25 December (Christmas Day)
26 December (St Stephen)
Each town keeps its patron saint's day as a holiday.

TELEPHONES

For all calls in Italy, dial the city code (for instance, 010 for Genoa), then the telephone number. For international and intercontinental calls, dial 00 before the telephone number. The country code for Italy is +39. In general, there is good mobile coverage in Liguria. Many hotels offer free WiFi: at reception they will typically ask you how many devices you want to use, and give you a user code for each. Smaller establishments have a single WiFi code that covers the whole premises.

TIPPING

Service charges are normally included and tipping in Italy is not routinely expected. It is normal to round up the bill and leave a few coins in appreciation

Index

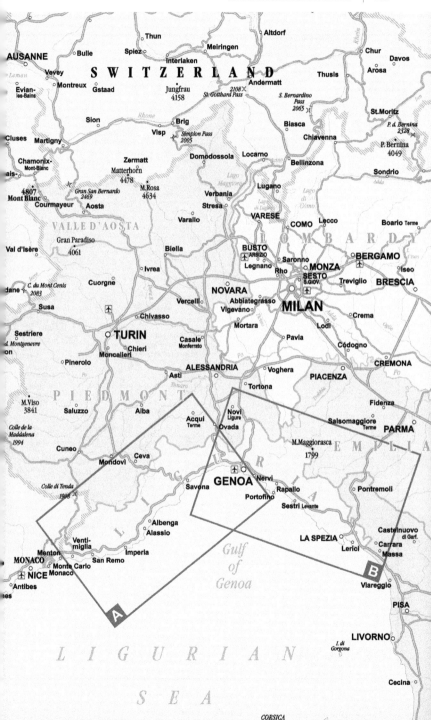

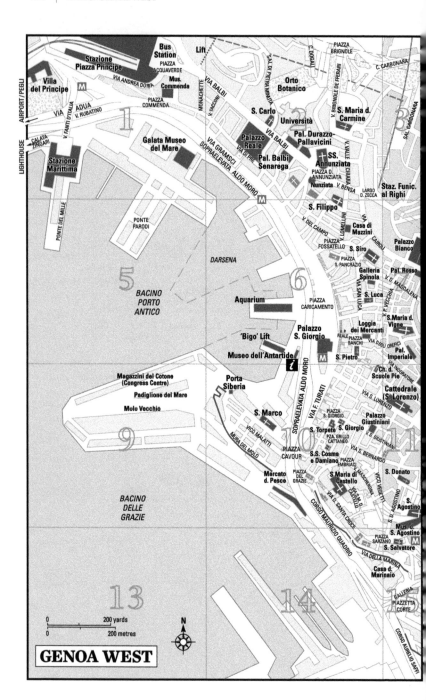

GENOA WEST

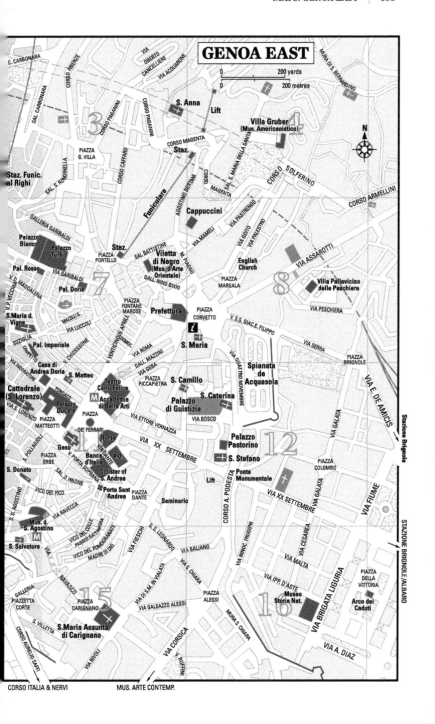

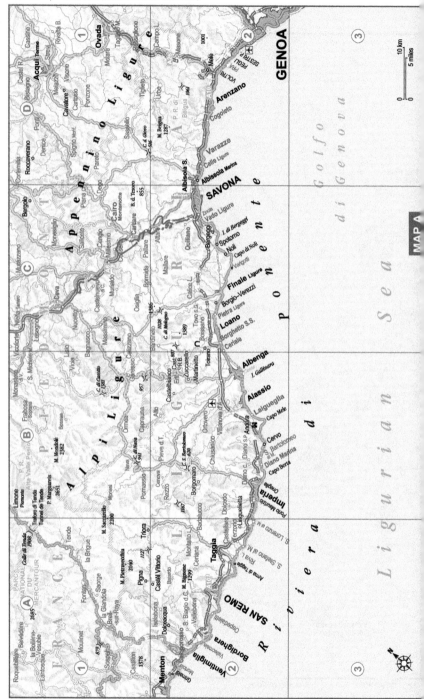

MAP A

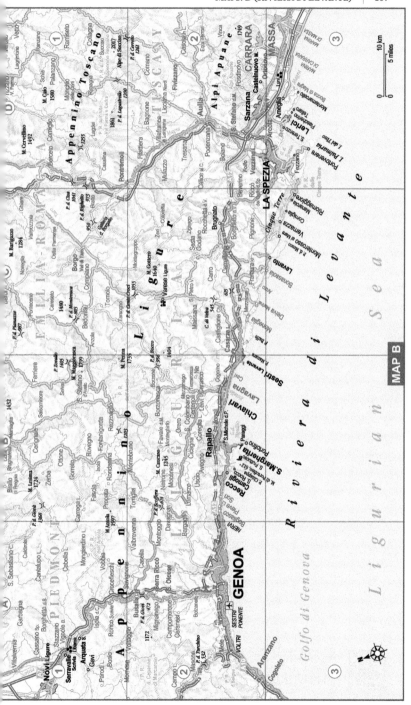

MAP B

Lightning Source UK Ltd.
Milton Keynes UK
UKHW022034070619
344049UK00013B/860/P